Jigsaw Puzzle Family

Jigsaw Puzzle Family

The Stepkids' Guide to Fitting It Together

Cynthia MacGregor

Impact 🌼 *Publishers*®
ATASCADERO, CALIFORNIA

ATTENTION ORGANIZATIONS AND CORPORATIONS:
This book is available at quantity discounts on bulk purchases for educational,
business, or sales promotional use. For further information, please contact
Impact Publishers, P.O. Box 6016, Atascadero, California 93423-6016.
Phone 805-466-5917, e-mail: info@impactpublishers.com

Barbie is a registered trademark of Mattel, Inc. *Parcheesi, Clue, Scrabble* and *Monopoly*
are registered trademarks of Hasbro, Inc.

Library of Congress Cataloging-in-Publication Data

MacGregor, Cynthia.
   Jigsaw puzzle family : the stepkids' guide to fitting it together / Cynthia
      MacGregor.-- 1st ed.
     p. cm. -- (Rebuilding books)
   Includes bibliographical references and index.
   ISBN 1-886230-63-3 (alk. paper)
     1. Stepchildren--Juvenile literature. 2. Stepfamilies--Juvenile literature.
   3. Divorced parents--Juvenile literature. 4. Stepparents--Juvenile literature.
   5. Children of divorced parents--Juvenile literature. I. Title. II. Rebuilding
   books, for divorce and beyond.

HQ777.7.M32 2005
306.874'7--dc22   2005001858

Publisher's Note
*This publication is designed to provide accurate and authoritative information in regard
to the subject matter covered. It is sold with the understanding that the publisher is not
engaged in rendering psychological, legal, or other professional services. If expert
assistance or counseling is needed, the services of a competent professional should be
sought.*

Impact Publishers and colophon are registered trademarks of Impact Publishers, Inc.

Cover by K.A. White Design, San Luis Obispo, California
Printed in the United States of America on acid-free paper.

Published by *Impact* 🕮 *Publishers*®
POST OFFICE BOX 6016
ATASCADERO, CALIFORNIA 93423-6016
www.impactpublishers.com

For all the kids who find themselves
feeling like puzzle pieces
that no longer quite fit
in the picture right...
for all the kids who wonder
how the jigsaw puzzle pieces
of their newly recombined family
will ever fit together...
in the hope this book
will help the family pieces
ease together better and faster

CONTENTS

Introduction

Jigsaw Puzzle Family? What do a *jigsaw puzzle* and a *family* have to do with each other? More than you might think, especially for all the people who are members of *stepfamilies.*

Since you're reading this book, chances are you've recently become — or are about to become — a part of what some people call a "blended family." A blended family is one that's made up of parts of one family and parts of another, all put together. Suppose, for example, that a divorced mom with one daughter marries a widowed dad with one son and one daughter. The result is a blended family.

Maybe you've seen reruns of *The Brady Bunch* series on Nick at Nite, or rented one of the movies about the TV family called the "Bradys." They are probably the world's best-known example of a "blended family."

Well, that's what a lot of psychologists and other people call them, but I think of them as "jigsaw puzzle families."

The individual pieces are supposed to fit together to make a big, pretty picture. The problem is, sometimes the pieces don't fit so perfectly well together. And sometimes the picture they make isn't quite as beautiful as you'd like.

How did you get to be part of a jigsaw puzzle family? You may have been born into one, but you most likely started out in a different family combination. Your mom and dad were probably married at one time. And then, either they got divorced or one of your parents died.

When that happened, unless you were very, very young, you probably felt like it was the end of the world. That's a normal feeling for kids when their parents' marriage ends. But after a while you began adjusting. You got used to living with just Mom or just Dad and maybe a sister or brother or two. If you stop and think hard, you can probably remember how you felt at first. When Dad or Mom left, you probably cried a lot, or just felt sad inside, or got angry pretty often. Or maybe you didn't feel much of anything. Sometimes we react to difficult times by just shutting down. We don't feel sad, but we don't feel happy either. We just... don't feel.

But after a while, things began to ease up. You still missed having Dad or Mom living in the house with you, but you began to get used to the new way things were. Right? Think about it. You had to work at accepting the changes and making the adjustment, and it probably happened slowly and gradually. You didn't just suddenly change. But, little by little, you became used to living with only one parent.

You also grew used to the other changes in your family. When a parent is widowed or divorced, there are always other changes. There may be less money. A mom who didn't work might now have to go to work. Maybe the family moved to a different house, or you started going to a different school.

After a while, things probably just didn't *seem* so bad anymore. It's not that things were actually any better or different, but you got used to the changes. If your parents got divorced, they didn't get back together. If one of them died… well, that's certainly not something that can change. But you gradually grew used to the new way things were. Right?

And then, some time later, Mom (or Dad) started dating. Maybe at first the dating didn't make too much of a difference in your life. But one day she (or he) told you she (or he) was going to get married again.

Pow! Suddenly there was a BIG impact on your life. At the very least, the remarriage of a parent means adding someone new into your world. And it definitely means the end of your hopes that your parents might get back together.

If the parent who's getting remarried is the parent you're not living with, the impact on you is less. If you live with your mom, for example, and it's your dad who gets married again, you're going to have a stepmother. But you won't be living with her, so you'll mostly feel the difference when you go to visit at Dad's house.

But maybe the parent who's remarrying is the parent you live with. Or maybe your parents have shared custody — you spend more or less the same amount of time with each of them. In either of these cases, you'll feel more changes.

To begin with, you'll have a new stepdad (or stepmom) living with you. If your new stepparent has one or more kids living with him or her, you'll now have a stepbrother or stepsister (or more than one) living with you, too. And even let's say your mom marries a man who has kids who don't live with him. They're still going to be around. Maybe they'll stay at your house on alternate weekends. Maybe they'll come for dinner on Wednesday nights. They may not live with you full time, but they're going to be spending time in your house. They're going to be part of your family. You're going to be dealing with sharing your mom or dad, and your new stepdad or stepmom, with them. Can you see the jigsaw puzzle pieces forming?

And talk about new people living with you... where *are* you going to live? That's another thing that might change. You and your mom might move into your new stepdad's house if it's larger (or for some other reason). Or your mom and stepdad and all the kids might move into a whole new house. Not your old house or your new stepdad's old house, but someplace new for all of you.

Suddenly you're going through a lot of changes! And very few people can go through major life changes without feeling them in some way. Some of us deal with change more easily than others do. But all changes — even good changes — need some getting used to.

And that's one of the messages of this book: You *will* get used to it. Just like you eventually got used to it when your parents divorced, or when one of your parents died. I don't promise that it will be easy. In fact, I can tell you there will be some rough times. But you *can* get used to being part of a new family arrangement. The puzzle pieces can fit together after a while.

In this book, we're going to talk about some of the situations you might find yourself facing. Some of them are good, but they'll still take some getting used to. Having two parents in the house again is good. But your new stepparent isn't the mom or dad you were born to, and you're not expected to love him or her right away. At first, in fact, it's going to feel kind of funny having him or her around. That's true even if you knew him or her pretty well before your mom or dad married him or her.

And just because he or she is different, that will take some getting used to too. Your new stepdad may have different rules from your dad's rules. Your new stepmom may be more huggy or less huggy than your mom, or think different things are important. (Your parent who just got married and your new stepparent may not always agree with each other, either.)

Some of the changes in your new life in your jigsaw puzzle family may not seem so good. If you have to share a room with a new stepsister or have a new stepbrother who's older than you and bosses you around, you may not think there's anything good about the situation.

Here's what this book can do for you:

• Reading the book will help you realize there are plenty of other kids who are going through the same things you are. Or they've gone through it already, and now they're used to the new way things are in their families. Knowing that other kids are dealing with similar situations may not actually make your situation different or better. But somehow it always seems to help to know you're not alone. It helps to know there are other kids going through all the same stuff.

• In cases where there is something you can actually do to make these changes easier, I'll make suggestions for how you can help make things better for you.

• Most of all, I want you to realize that, even when there's nothing you can do to help make things feel more happy for you, time will help. In time you'll get used to the way things are. You may not think so now, but it's true. Remember I asked you to think back to how it was when your parents first divorced or one of your parents died? Think about it again, now. Think about how, after a while, you got used to the way things were. You still miss having both your parents living with you, but you *have* become used to it. It doesn't hurt nearly as much. The same thing is true about being part of a stepfamily. Whether you believe it or not, you *will* get used to having a new stepparent, having new rules in the house, perhaps having new stepbrothers or stepsisters, perhaps living somewhere new too.

Now let's take a look at some of the situations you might find yourself dealing with in your new jigsaw puzzle family. Ready?

1

Mixed Emotions

▼ ▼ ▼

Jenny had always been an "only" child, so when her parents got divorced, it was just Jenny and her mom in the house. Jenny's mom tried to pay extra attention to her, to make up for Jenny's dad not living there anymore. And at dinner, and during the evening after that, Jenny's mom talked to Jenny a lot... more than she ever had before.

Jenny liked having her mom pay so much attention to her. But she didn't like the fact that her mom was always fussing over her and asking lots of questions. Her mom asked her more questions now than she ever used to. She asked about school, about Jenny's friends, about whether Jenny had been dressed warmly enough that day, *everything*.

Jenny's mom had always been interested in how school had been, and whether everything was OK with Jenny. But she had never asked *so many* questions. Jenny was glad her mom loved her. She was glad that her mom cared enough to be worried about her. But sometimes she wished her mom would just *leave her alone!*

Then, after about half a year, Jenny's mom started going out on dates. And another four months later, she met someone she really liked. His name was Jim, and Jenny's mom started seeing him a lot.

Now Jenny's mom wasn't home for dinner some nights. And even when Jenny's mom *was* home, she didn't talk to Jenny quite as much as she had or ask her so many questions. Even though Jenny didn't understand exactly what this had to do with Jim, she could see that that was when it had started. It was just when Jenny's mom started seeing Jim that she had stopped drowning Jenny in so many questions and talking to her so much.

Then one day, Jenny's mom announced that she and Jim were going to get married! Even before that, Jenny had been feeling pretty uncomfortable about the time her mom was spending with Jim. Now her emotions were really mixed up... as if she felt two different things at once. On the one hand, she was grateful that her mother had stopped asking such a huge number of questions. On the other hand, she missed all the attention from her mom.

Jenny felt annoyed at her mom for paying less attention to her. She also felt annoyed at herself because she didn't think it was right to feel annoyed at her mom. And all these mixed-up feelings only made Jenny feel worse than ever.

Jenny's mom didn't have as much time for Jenny now, either. She was spending a lot of time with Jim. Sometimes they did things with Jenny. Sometimes they did things just by themselves while Jenny was at a friend's house, at home, or at a school activity. And sometimes Jenny's mom was busy with Jim when Jenny wanted Mom to be with *her*. It used to be that Mom took her places. Now it *seemed* Mom didn't have time to pay much attention to her.

Jenny had different kinds of feelings about Jim, too. All at the same time, she liked him and she objected to him. All at the same time she appreciated him and resented him.

Why?

Well, for one thing, Jim was really basically a nice man. And he treated Jenny nicely. On the other hand, it felt as if he was trying to push his way into the family. Was he trying to take her dad's place? Jenny really resented that.

Things had been comfortable when it was just Jenny and her mom. She didn't want anyone else messing things up. She liked the way things were before.

But yet, Jenny was actually grateful that Jim had taken up some of her mother's attention. Now that Mom wasn't asking her so many questions all the time, Jenny was happier.

Still, Jenny understood that it was because of Jim that she wasn't so much the center of her mom's life anymore. And Jenny resented him for that.

So Jenny had lots of feelings tugging against each other. She was grateful, she was upset, she was happy, she was disappointed... and she was all these things all at once! To top it all off, she was annoyed at herself for even having all these different feelings fighting with each other inside her.

▲ ▲ ▲

It's understandable that Jenny would be confused by so many different feelings. But really, they're all perfectly natural. We all like to be the center of attention. We all like feeling we're very important to someone, whether it's a relative or a friend. Yet, when parents ask question after question after question, it can sometimes leave a kid feeling annoyed. So it's no wonder that Jenny feels such different feelings at the same time.

The first thing Jenny needs to do is accept what she's feeling. It's perfectly normal to feel the way she does. And, even though it seems that the two things she's feeling contradict each other, they don't. Jenny likes getting a lot of her mother's attention; she just doesn't like getting so many questions.

Her feelings are normal. Her feelings are understandable. And in time, Jenny will get used to the change in how things are in her family. Now that Jenny's mom is getting married again, she'll have another adult in the family. There will be someone else in the house for Mom to talk to, and Jenny will get a little less of her attention. (This would be true if Jenny's mom had another child, too.) In fact, things will probably be kind of the way they were when Jenny's dad was still living with Jenny and her mom. And Jenny will get used to it again. She'll have to give it some time, and she'll have to learn to adjust, but she'll be OK.

Talk to Somebody!

It would be a good idea for Jenny to discuss her feelings with her mom if she can. If it's too hard to talk with her mom about it, maybe she can share her feelings with a friend, her grandmother, or a teacher in school who she feels understands her. If you find yourself in a situation like Jenny's, talking it out with someone will help.

If you have a friend who's "been there, done that," by all means talk to that friend. It could even be good to talk to someone you know and trust and get along with who has been through a parent's remarriage, even if he or she is not a really close friend. This might be a classmate, a neighbor, the son or daughter of one of your mom's friends, or some other kid you know. Even if your best friend has not lived through her parents' remarriage, however, it will help if you talk your feelings over with her. Talking it out with someone you trust helps!

And that suggestion is true of all the situations in this book. Talking to someone who's been through the same thing you're going through is usually your best bet. But it's helpful to talk out the situation and your feelings with *anyone* you trust to listen well.

Keeping a journal can be helpful too. Sometimes just getting your feelings down on paper can help you.

Who Do You Love?

When a parent remarries, there are lots of changes in the family. What Jenny went through is one example. There are other differences when a parent remarries, too. And sometimes it's harder to get used to these new situations than others. Check out Rob's story.

▼ ▼ ▼

Rob's parents got divorced when Rob was five years old. When he was seven, his dad moved out to California. Since Rob and his mom and sister lived in Iowa, that meant he didn't get to see his dad very often.

Rob flew out to California that first Christmas after his dad moved. Rob got to spend the holiday seeing Hollywood, which was almost as exciting as seeing his dad again. And after that, he flew out to see his dad every Christmas vacation, every Easter vacation, and a part of every summer vacation.

But in between times, he missed his dad. And it wasn't only that Rob missed his dad in general. There were specific times when Rob really wished his dad lived nearer, even if Dad and Mom weren't married anymore. Like when his Sunday School held their annual Father-Son Dinner, and Rob didn't have a father to go with. Or when he went to Little League and saw that most of the boys were there with their dads.

Rob was ten when his mom met Sean. Sean was a nice man, and Rob really liked him. When Rob's mom told Rob and his sister that she was going to marry Sean, Rob was really happy for her. He even escorted his mom down the aisle at the wedding.

Rob was happy for himself too. It was nice to have a man living in the house again. Sean and Rob talked about guy things. Rob found that Sean gave him good advice.

Sean had begun taking Rob and his sister to see baseball games. When the circus came to town, Sean took the two kids to the circus. And Sean started coming to some of Rob's Little League games too.

And then, one day at one of the games, Rob felt a sudden sharp feeling of guilt. Rob had hit a triple. He slid into third base just a second ahead of the ball! "Yesss!" That was Sean's voice, cheering from the stands. Sean was yelling and screaming for Rob. He was as proud of him as if Rob were his own kid.

Rob realized that. Standing right there on third base, slapping the dust off his uniform, Rob realized it. Sean was as proud of Rob as if Rob were his own son. And Rob suddenly felt two different feelings at once. He felt proud and happy. And at the same time, he felt guilty.

Rob wasn't just proud of having hit that triple. He was proud that Sean was proud of him. He felt good that Sean was there cheering for him. It was nice to have somebody kind of like a dad to yell and cheer for him, and to show him how to hit the ball better. Rob was sure that Sean's coaching him at home had helped him to be able to hit that triple.

But suddenly Rob felt guilty! He thought about his own dad, out in California. *Dad* should have been there to see Rob hit that triple. *Dad* should be up in the stands, cheering. And Rob should be enjoying his victory with Dad... not with Sean.

Rob felt disloyal. And it wasn't just about softball. Rob suddenly realized that he liked Sean. He enjoyed being with Sean and doing things with Sean. And he felt wrong. He felt it was wrong to enjoy Sean, to like Sean. He felt he was being disloyal to his dad.

▲ ▲ ▲

Rob really has nothing to feel guilty about, yet we can understand that he feels the way he does. As he begins to love and appreciate Sean, it's normal for him to think he's being disloyal to his dad. It isn't really a case of loving one or the other more. Rob can love *both* Dad and Sean. And Sean is very important to Rob, since Dad isn't living nearby. With Dad far away, it's great that Sean is there — both emotionally and physically — to support Rob.

Rob has the right to enjoy himself at a Little League game. Rob has the right to enjoy having someone like a dad in the family to talk to, to get advice from, and to do things with. Rob has the right to like and even love his stepdad. And the sooner he accepts this fact, the sooner he'll get over feeling guilty. While it's perfectly understandable that he feels guilty, it's completely unnecessary. *Rob hasn't done anything to feel guilty about.*

Loving Sean and appreciating Sean doesn't mean that Rob loves his dad any less. It doesn't mean he doesn't wish his dad were there to see him. But his dad *isn't* there. And there's nothing wrong with being glad *someone* is there to watch Rob do well at the game and cheer for him. There's nothing wrong with enjoying Sean's company. There's nothing disloyal about liking Sean — or even *loving* him.

Love isn't an either–or thing. Love isn't something we have only so much of. Rob is perfectly capable of loving both his dad *and* Sean. He doesn't have to choose between them. Rob has enough love in him for his mom, his sister, his dad, his new stepdad, *and* his other relatives, plus a few other people he particularly cares about.

Rob's dad never said to him, "Who do you love; me or Sean?" Rob's dad never even said to him, "Who do you love *more*; me or Sean?" (And that would be an unfair question to ask!) Rob's problem sprang up inside himself. It's not because of anything his dad said to him. It's not because of anything his mom or sister or anyone said, either. Rob just started to feel guilty on his own.

It's understandable. It's common. But it's unnecessary. Lots of kids feel this way when they realize they've grown to like (or even love) their new stepdads or stepmoms. But it's not necessary. This isn't a competition. There's not a contest between a mom and a stepmom or a dad and a stepdad. It's perfectly all right to like and love both.

Learning to Love Another Mother

▼ ▼ ▼

Tara is in a situation that's like Rob's in some ways. Tara's mom, Nancy, died a few years ago. Tara's dad met a nice woman last year, and after a while he introduced her to Tara. The woman's name is Sara, and she made jokes with Tara about their names. "Tara and Sara. We're almost alike. Our names are so similar."

In fact, Tara and Sara have a lot in common, and Tara gets along really well with Sara. Tara's dad married Sara, and Tara was glad to have a "new mom." She even started calling Sara "Mom."

But then her Aunt Liz heard Tara call Sara "Mom."
Aunt Liz got upset.

"You mustn't do that. You had a mom. Sara's your
stepmother. You shouldn't call her 'Mom'," Aunt Liz
told Tara. She made Tara feel guilty about loving Sara
and calling her "Mom."

Tara stopped calling Sara "Mom." She stopped
snuggling with her in the evenings. In fact, she
wouldn't even let Sara kiss her goodnight anymore.
She insisted her dad tuck her in instead.

Tara felt bad inside. She missed the closeness with
Sara. She missed the love she felt. But her Aunt Liz
made Tara feel that she was being disloyal to her first
mom by loving Sara and by calling Sara "Mom."

▼ ▼ ▼

Aunt Liz was wrong! But you already know that grown-ups
can be wrong sometimes. You already know that grown-ups
sometimes make mistakes. And Aunt Liz was making a
mistake; she was being very unfair to Tara.

Aunt Liz missed Tara's mom too. She and Nancy had been
sisters. And it hurt Liz to see that Tara was letting someone
else take her sister's place. Liz would never have another
sister. And it hurt her to see that Tara was accepting another
woman as her mom.

But Aunt Liz was very wrong.

Tara still loved her mom — her original mom — very
much. But Tara's mom is dead now. Tara hadn't turned away
from her. Nancy is gone, and Sara is good to Tara, and Sara
is good *for* Tara. It's certainly a good thing for a girl to have
a mom when she's growing up. And Sara, Tara's stepmom,
was happy to be Tara's second mom.

There's nothing wrong with that!

Accepting Sara as a stepmother — a second mother — and even calling her "Mom" didn't take away from how much Tara loved her first mom. And it didn't make Tara love Nancy any less. But Tara's birth mom (the mom she was born to) is dead.

It's fine for Tara to love Sara, just as she loves her dad, and Aunt Liz, and all three of her living grandparents. Tara — just like Rob — has plenty of love to go around for everyone in her family!

Tara needs to understand that. It might help her if she talked to her dad. Certainly her dad loved Nancy. Certainly her dad still misses her. But now he has grown to love Sara. If Tara talks to Dad, maybe he can help her understand that it's all right to learn to love someone else — that it isn't disrespectful to her birth mom. Tara needs to be able to accept the fact that it's OK for her to love Sara. If she reads books like this one, and others on the subject, maybe that will help her too.

It's possible that Tara feels guilty because she doesn't think about her mom or miss her as much as she used to. Think about this: One of your parents no longer lives with you. And you miss him or her. (For now, let's say it's your mom.) You miss all the things you loved about your mom. And you miss the things you used to do with your mom.

What is there about your mom herself that you miss? Her funny jokes? The way she always seemed to understand what was bothering you? The way she could always make you feel better with a hug? The goofy things she did? She — and all these things that made her special — are gone.

What is there that your mom used to do with you that you miss? Did she sing a special silly song when she kissed you goodnight? Did she wash your hair extra-gently? Did she tuck I-love-you notes into your lunchbox? Did she take you for walks on the beach in the middle of winter?

Now suppose your dad gets married again. And suppose Dad's new wife — your stepmom — sings a song when she kisses you goodnight. (Maybe it's not the *same* song your mom sang, but it's a good one.) Maybe she washes your hair much more gently than Dad does. Maybe she tucks funny animal pictures into your pockets for you to find, and she draws a heart on them because she loves you. And maybe one day you told her how Mom used to take you to the beach in the winter, and now your stepmom does that too.

You still miss your mom. You miss the person she was. But you don't have to miss all that other good stuff anymore. Your stepmom is singing to you now, and beach-walking with you in the winter, and all those other things.

Suddenly you realize you don't miss your mom as much as you used to.

You still miss *her*. You just don't have to miss *the things you did together.* You have someone else to do them with now. If you stop to think about it, you'll realize it's not *your mom* you miss less. It's only *things*. When Tara stops to think about it, she'll realize, too, that she still loves and misses her mom. She just doesn't have to miss as many *things.* Tara needs to believe that she's not being disrespectful to her mother's memory. Not even if she calls Sara "Mom." Nancy would be happy to know someone else is taking good care of the daughter she loved so much.

Tara has mixed emotions, just like Rob and Jenny do. She wants to be loyal to her birth mom, but she likes and loves Sara and wants Sara for a mom now. There's nothing wrong with that. She can love both moms. She doesn't have to choose.

Her father would help her, if she would go to him and tell him what the problem is. (She could also ask to speak to the school counselor or psychologist. Or she could talk to her clergyperson — her minister, priest, rabbi, or cantor. Or she could talk to a teacher she trusts.) And hopefully, she'll soon accept the fact that it's really, really, really all right for her to love Sara and accept her as a new mom.

If you have a stepparent you love, please don't feel guilty about it! (And that's true whether one of your parents has died or if both your parents are alive but divorced from each other.) Love is something we all have an unlimited supply of. Loving your stepmother doesn't mean you don't love your mother. And loving your stepmother more and more doesn't mean loving your mother less and less. You have enough love in you to go around.

"Hey, You!" (What Do You Call a Stepparent?)
Kids who aren't comfortable calling a stepparent "Mom" or "Dad" shouldn't have to call them that. But if you *want* to call your new stepmother "Mom," or if you *want* to call your new stepfather "Dad," that's perfectly all right, as long as it's comfortable for you and for the stepparent.

What are some of the other things you can call a stepparent?

Many stepparents don't object to being called by their first names. If your stepdad's name is "Alan," maybe he'll be comfortable if you just call him by his name: "Alan." Or maybe you could call him, "Pop Alan" or "Papa Alan."

Sometimes one of these other names for a father works by itself, like "Papa." "Dad" could be what you call your birth dad, and "Papa" could be what you call your stepdad.

Or if it's your dad who's remarried, so you now have a stepmother, you could call her by her name — let's say that's "Elaine." Or she could be "Mom Elaine." Or your birth mom could be "Mom" and Elaine could be "Mama."

You might even have a cute or funny nickname you call a stepparent by. In one jigsaw puzzle family, the stepmom — whose name is Liz — is called "MyLiz" by her stepkids.

What's even more important than what you call these people, though, is what you feel about them. You need to feel comfortable with them. You need to feel free to love them if you want to.

And you need to get adjusted to all the other changes that come with a new stepparent in the house. New rules. Sometimes new foods. Sometimes new brothers and sisters, too.

We'll talk about all these things in the rest of this book.

Points to Remember

• *It's OK to love both your parent and your stepparent.*

• *Loving your stepparent more doesn't mean loving your birth parent less.*

• *You might stop missing the things you did with your absent parent. This is true if you're now doing them with someone else — a stepparent, your other parent, your grandma…. But no longer missing things doesn't mean you no longer miss your absent parent.*

• *It's OK to call your stepparent "Mom" or "Dad." And it's also OK not to call them "Mom" or "Dad."*

2

Life Turns Upside-Down

▼ ▼ ▼

Sometimes life just doesn't seem fair, at least according to Ryan. Like many people, Ryan doesn't handle changes easily. When he was four, his father was transferred by his job. Ryan's family had to move. Ryan had to get used to a new house, a new neighborhood, a new town, a new pre-school, new kids to play with.

Well, he finally got used to all that. But when Ryan was seven, his parents got divorced. First Ryan had to get used to Dad not living with Ryan and his mom anymore. Then Ryan and his sister and his mom moved. His mom said she couldn't afford the big house anymore. They moved to a small apartment. Ryan had to get used to *that*. It wasn't easy moving again. And it wasn't easy living in an apartment with no back yard.

Then — as if Ryan hadn't seen enough of his life change already — his mom told him she was getting married again. Ryan was going to have a new stepdad named Karl. Not only that, but Karl had two kids of his own, and they'd be spending some weekends and some other times with Ryan and his mom and Karl.

Karl is a nice enough man, and Ryan and he got along fine from the beginning. Karl told Ryan that, since he already has a dad, he could call Karl "Pop K" ("K" for "Karl"), so Ryan went on calling his birth dad "Dad" and started calling his new stepdad "Pop K."

But it felt so weird to Ryan to have someone else besides his sister living with him and his mom again. And of course he and his mom moved again, so Ryan had to get used to another new neighborhood and another new school.

So many changes! Ryan wasn't sure how he could handle it!

He started worrying about it a lot. In school, instead of paying attention to the teacher, he sat at his desk and worried. He worried about the situation at home, and about making friends with the new kids in the neighborhood and in school. He worried about having to share his mom's time again. He worried a lot. His teacher noticed that he wasn't paying attention. She asked him, "Is something wrong?" But because he had just met her, he didn't feel as if he could tell her what was bothering him.

And then there were Karl's kids to deal with, too. The four-year-old girl was OK, though she seemed kind of like a baby to Ryan. The six-year-old boy was younger than Ryan too, but Ryan and Mikey were able to find things to do together, so mostly that was all right.

But there were many times when Ryan just wanted to be alone, yet Mikey wouldn't leave him alone. Mikey wanted company. Mikey wanted to throw a ball around. Mikey wanted to talk. Mikey wanted to play computer games. And sometimes Ryan just wanted to be by himself.

"Be nice to your new stepbrother," Mom said. But when Ryan wrote email to his friends, he called Mikey his new "stepbother." It seemed all Mikey did was bother Ryan.

Sometimes Ryan lost his temper and yelled, "Can't you just leave me alone?" But when Mikey put his head down and walked away, Ryan felt worse instead of better.

It was just too many changes. Ryan was having trouble dealing with them all.

▲ ▲ ▲

Changes are difficult even for an adult. Too many changes at once, or too many changes in a row, are tough for anyone to handle. Ryan needs to concentrate on the things that aren't changing. Maybe it would help him if he started by making a list. He could list all the things that have stayed the same and are going to keep on staying the same:

• His dad is still his dad, and always will be, no matter who lives where.

• His mom is still his mom, and Ryan and his mom still live together, regardless of who else lives there full-time or part-time. That's not likely to change, either, at least not till Ryan grows up and moves out.

• His parents both still love him and always will.

• He has the same grandparents, uncles, aunts, and cousins. And they won't change.

• His friendships are solid. He has the same good friends, and that isn't going to change.

• He still has all his games, toys, books, and music. He still has his computer (and some email friends). He still enjoys doing all the same things he always did, from computer games to reading to softball to building model cars.

If he made a list, he'd realize just how much of his life *hasn't* changed and isn't likely to. It might be some comfort to him to think about that.

Also, although his parents may be making decisions without consulting him, there are things he *can* control in his life — what he wears to school, what sports he plays, whether to try out for school band, how to decorate his room, whether to do scouts or 4-H or summer camp — so he'll find he really is in charge of some of his life.

It would also be a good thing if Ryan's mom would spend some time together with just him on a regular basis. Not with Karl, not with Karl's kids… just Ryan and his mom. They could go out for pizza together, or bowl a line or two at the local bowling alley, or go jogging, or do most anything that Ryan enjoys and that they could do together.

And they should definitely choose someplace where they can *talk*.

It would be good if Ryan's mom would think of this herself, but if she doesn't, Ryan could suggest it to her. He needs to speak up. After all, his mom is going through a lot of changes in her life too. She might not realize how Ryan feels.

Ryan needs to tell her, "Mom, I want to spend more time alone with you, like we used to."

Mom will probably tell him, "We can't spend as much time alone together as we used to. There are more people in the family now." And that's true.

But if Ryan speaks up for himself, he could answer, "I know. But sometimes I need to spend more time with just you than we're doing now."

If Ryan could count on spending time alone with his mom once a week, he would certainly feel a lot better about the way so many things in his life seem to be changing.

Room for One More?

▼ ▼ ▼

Jack had always had his own room, but then his mom married Papa Pete. Jack got along well with his new stepdad, and he didn't object too much to his new stepbrother. Kyle was five years younger than Jack, and sometimes he was kind of a pain in the butt, but basically he was all right. There was just one problem: For the first time in his life, Jack had to share his room. Jack had a sister, Sherri, but she had always had her own room and Jack had had his own room.

Papa Pete was a widower — his first wife had died — so Kyle lived with him all the time, not just weekends. When Papa Pete and Jack's mom got married, Papa Pete and Kyle moved into the family's three-bedroom house. Jack's mom explained that, since Jack and Kyle were both boys, they would have to share a bedroom.

"It's not fair!" Jack complained loudly. "Let him share with Sherri!"

"You're both boys. Let him share with you," Jack's mom said. But Jack wasn't happy with that at all!

Jack made a big fuss, and his mother got upset with him. "I'm sorry," she said, "but that's the way things are. Your room is the most logical place for Kyle. Carrying on and yelling like that doesn't change matters any. In fact, I'm disappointed in you.

"I understand how you feel. I really do," she added, "but sometimes in this world we have to put up with situations we're not happy about. As you get older, you'll learn that."

"I hate Papa Pete and Kyle!" Jack yelled in a stormy voice.

"No, you don't," his mother said softly. "And I know you don't mean that. You're just angry. And I understand why you're angry. But you'll have to get over it. This is the way things are. And I know you're old enough to understand."

Jack went to his room and slammed the door. He kicked the furniture. He tore a poster off the wall and ripped it up. It was a picture of his favorite singer, but Papa Pete had given it to him, and right now he was angry at Papa Pete. He took it out on the poster. He ripped it to shreds.

After a while, though, Jack calmed down. He lay on his bed and thought. He thought about what his mom said about him being old enough to understand. And he thought that, if he was old enough to understand, maybe he was old enough for some more privileges, too.

Finally he went back downstairs. "Mom?" he asked.

"Yes, honey?" his mother answered.

"If I'm getting older — old enough to understand things, like you said — then I think I'm old enough to go to bed half an hour later."

His mother laughed, but she didn't say no. "I'll think about it," she said.

"There's something else," Jack said.

"What?" his mom asked.

"It's gotten pretty crowded in my room with Kyle in there too. And I need a place to do my homework. Would you buy me a desk and put it in the living room like your desk is?"

His mom laughed. "If we can find room for it in the living room, I think that would be OK. It's pretty crowded in there now with Papa Pete's recliner in there."

"But Dad's easel used to be in the living room," Jack pointed out. His dad liked to paint for a hobby, and he had done his painting in the living room. "It's not any more crowded now than it was when the easel was there."

Jack didn't whine. He didn't make a scene. He spoke to his mom calmly. And she listened. The next weekend, she and Papa Pete did some rearranging of the living room furniture. Then they went out and bought a small but sturdy desk for Jack. When Jack thanked his mom for the desk, he remembered to thank Papa Pete, too. Later, as he was getting ready to go to bed, Jack thanked his mom for the second time. "See you tomorrow," he said, kissing her good-night.

"You don't have to go to bed yet," his mom said. "Your bedtime is a half-hour later now."

▲ ▲ ▲

Jack is lucky. He has a mom who understood what he was feeling. Most moms understand a lot of what's going on in their kids' heads. But nobody can get it right all the time. And when kids scream and carry on, it doesn't help their moms to understand. It doesn't help them get what they want, either.

Jack got what he wanted — a desk in the living room and a later bedtime — not only because his mom understood what he was feeling, but also because of Jack himself. When Jack calmed down, he told his mom what he wanted. He didn't fuss. He didn't demand. He didn't get angry or whine or cry. He talked calmly. And his mom listened.

Jack also needs to learn to live with having a new younger brother; Kyle is a part of his family now. New younger siblings want to be just like you. Try to take it as a compliment! His new stepbrother is going through tough changes too, and it will be best for Jack to try to understand Kyle so he won't regret later how he treats him. He'll need to set some boundaries with Kyle — limits about time and space together — that are fair for both of them.

Parents often understand what their kids are going through at times like these. Even a new stepdad or stepmom who's wonderful still brings a change in your life. And big changes — like big jigsaw puzzles — are sometimes tough to deal with. But when your mom or dad doesn't understand what's going on, it's up to *you* to get the message through. Not by whining. Not by stamping your feet. Not by yelling. Not by being difficult. *Talk.*

You may not always understand your own feelings. It helps if you can figure them out. It will help your parents understand what you're going through. It will help you, too. If *you* understand what you're feeling, and what you're upset about, it's the first step to feeling better.

Talk to a friend. Talk to an adult you trust — a teacher you like, or a friend's mom or dad whom you feel comfortable with. Write your feelings down on paper, if that helps you. But try to be calm about it. Don't demand. Don't make a fuss. Talk it out.

Points to Remember

• *One of the reasons that becoming part of a stepfamily may be difficult is that it involves a lot of changes. Changes are difficult for many people.*

• *If it seems your world is changing too much, try making a list of all the things that haven't changed. List everything that's still the same.*

• *If there's something that would make you feel better, ask for it. Speak up for what you want. You may not get it, but it's worth asking for. But don't whine or cry or yell or demand. Ask. And you'll improve your chances if you ask nicely.*

3

Where Do I Fit In?

▼ ▼ ▼

Zac was always an only child — till a year after his
parents split up. Zac was eight at the time his parents
got divorced. His parents and the judge at the
divorce hearing all agreed that Zac should live with
his dad.

Everything went along reasonably well for quite a
while. Of course it was difficult for Zac not to live in
the same house with his mom anymore. He missed
her. He saw her twice a week, except when she was
traveling on business. But he still missed her tucking
him in at night, cooking his favorite meals for him,
and just being there.

Still, Zac and his dad were really close. Zac's dad
wasn't a bad cook, and it turned out that Dad could
make up some really funny stories to tell Zac at
bedtime. Zac had thought he was too old for

bedtime stories, but his dad's stories really made him laugh! He enjoyed them a lot!

Then Zac's dad starting dating. And after a while, he met a woman he really liked. Ellen was nice to Zac, and she cooked some of his favorite meals. She was great at helping him with his homework. She also was really good at helping him figure out what to do when he had a problem.

But she couldn't help him with his biggest problem, and that was Linus. Linus was Ellen's son. He was kind of a goofy kid a year and a half younger than Zac. A lot of times, when Ellen would come over to visit Zac and his dad, she brought Linus with her.

Zac's dad expected Zac to be a good host and make Linus feel at home in their house. Dad expected Zac to hang out with Linus and do things with him like play videogames and stuff. But Linus and Zac didn't like doing any of the same things, and Zac didn't enjoy spending time with him.

When Dad told Zac that he was going to marry Ellen, Zac asked, "What about Linus?"

"It's a package deal," his dad answered. "We'll all be a family."

Zac didn't like that very much. And when Ellen and Linus moved in, it was just as bad as he'd been afraid it would be. Dad and Ellen expected Zac to be a big brother to Linus. But Zac didn't feel like Linus's brother. He didn't love Linus. He didn't even particularly *like* Linus.

"It's not that I hate him or anything," Zac tried to explain to Dad one night. "But I don't feel like he's my brother. And we have nothing in common."

"Try your best," was all Dad said. "Just try to be nice to him. Think of how he feels in a strange house. And you're just as different from him as he is from you.

"Besides," Dad said, "I think part of your problem is just not being an 'only' child anymore. You were used to having me and Mom all to yourself. Then, after the divorce, you had me all to yourself and didn't even have to share me with Mom. Now you not only have to share me with Ellen, but you have to share me with Linus, too."

▲ ▲ ▲

Love can't be forced. And nobody can make a rule, "You will love your new stepbrother." But Zac's dad had a point. In fact, he had made several good points.

First of all, he was right that Zac wasn't used to sharing him. It was difficult for Zac. And when he calmed down and thought about it, he realized Dad was right.

And that wasn't all Dad was right about. As bad as Zac felt about having Linus there, he realized that Linus probably felt even worse. At least Zac was still living in his old, familiar house. Linus not only had a new stepdad and a new stepbrother, he also was living in a new house and going to a new school.

Once Zac thought about things from Linus's point of view, he started feeling more sympathetic to Linus. They still didn't have any interests in common, but they did have *something* in common. They were both in a similar situation

— having to suddenly share a parent with a new stepparent *and* a new stepbrother. And they both had been used to being "only" children and not sharing their parents with another kid.

If you find yourself in a similar situation, remember, it's at least as tough on the other kid, and maybe even tougher. Stop and think: Is it really true that you have nothing in common? Or are you just too busy resenting your new stepbrother or stepsister for you to realize what you *do* have in common?

Even if you really don't have any interests in common, you do share a situation. You do share the need to adjust to it. Realize that your new stepbrother or stepsister is in the same uncomfortable situation you are. But you may be able to help each other. You can't change the fact that your families have now merged together. You *can* change the way you look at that fact. You *can* change your attitude toward your stepfamily.

You have a choice. You can sit and stew and resent the way things are, or you can deal with it. You can get over it. Remarrying was your parent's choice. Your attitude is *your* choice. You can't make yourself love your new stepbrother or stepsister; you *can* learn to accept and tolerate him or her. And in time, you may even come to love him or her.

Give it a chance. Love doesn't happen overnight. But in time — who knows?! You might find — even if the two of you have absolutely nothing in common — that you really *like* the kid. And after a while, you may be surprised to realize one day that you've grown to love him or her.

Putting the Pieces Together

▼ ▼ ▼

Seth was the oldest of the three kids in his family. As a result, he had more privileges, a later bedtime than the others, and more responsibility. He liked being the oldest. And yes, he sometimes bossed his younger brother and sister around.

Then his parents divorced. When his mom met a widower named Gary, Seth wasn't particularly unhappy. "Watch. I'll bet they get married," he predicted to his brother and sister. He felt very smart for knowing what was likely to happen.

But he wasn't quite as smart as he thought. He didn't realize *everything* that was going to happen.

Gary had two sons. One was less than a year younger than Seth. He and Seth got along great. They liked the same games, the same books, the same music. Erik was easygoing and easy to get along with.

Gary's other son was Matthew. Matthew was two years older than Seth. Matthew and Seth didn't have as much in common, but they seemed to get along OK.

Then, just as Seth had said, his mom and Gary got married. The combined family moved into a larger house. They needed more space! Well, that part was all right. What wasn't all right was that now Matthew was the oldest kid in this new, combined family.

Suddenly Seth was no longer at the top of the heap. Suddenly he wasn't the one bossing everyone. He wasn't the one who had the most privileges. He wasn't the one who had the latest bedtime. Now that was Matthew, and Seth resented it.

Now Matthew told Seth what to do. "You're not the boss of me," Seth told him.

But Matthew said, "Yes, I am. I'm older."

Seth complained to his mom, but she just said, "You and Matthew have to learn to get along. You're brothers now. We're all one family."

Seth found himself bossing around his younger brother and sister more than ever — and Erik too.

Finally, Seth's own sister complained to Gary about Seth. Gary talked to Seth, then called a family meeting. Nobody was happy about going to another meeting, but everybody showed up.

"You all have to lighten up," Gary said. "This isn't about who can be the bossiest. This isn't about who's in charge. This isn't about who can be top dog. Matthew? Seth? Do you both understand me?"

"Yes, Dad," Matthew said, although it sounded like he didn't mean it.

"Yes, Gary," Seth said. But he gave his sister a look that would have withered a watermelon.

"That's good. Now listen," Gary said. "It's not easy being part of a new family. It's not easy giving up your position as the oldest." He looked at Seth. "But every situation has both bad and good. Do you like being Erik's brother?"

Seth nodded his head. "Sometimes," he said quietly.

"Do you and Erik get along? Do you enjoy hanging out with him?"

Seth nodded his head again, "Mostly."

"Me too!" Erik said.

Seth smiled for the first time since the meeting had started.

"Then I suggest you think about the good sides to this new family situation. And as for you, Matthew, lighten up! You don't have to boss Seth around just to show you're the oldest. We all know what your position is. Don't abuse it... or you'll lose privileges."

"Yes, Dad," Matthew said.

"Seth?"

"What?"

"If you think Matthew — or anyone else in the family — is being unfair to you, bring it to your mom or me. Don't try to solve it yourself. Don't take it out on your sister or brothers. Do you understand?"

"Yes, Gary. But... "

"No buts. Everyone has problems... even when they're not part of a whole new family. Everybody in the world has problems. But if you have a problem and you can't work it out yourself, you need to talk it out. And that's one of the things parents are for — to help their kids with their problems. If you can't solve a problem yourself, take it to your parents. Don't take it out on someone else. And be honest with yourself and with your parents about what the problem is. OK?"

▲ ▲ ▲

What can you do if you find yourself in a situation like Seth's? Actually, there are several possibilities. One is to ask your parents for a family meeting. At family meetings you can bring up complaints. You can ask for help with situations you can't work out yourself. It's not being a tattletale to bring a gripe to a meeting. That's better than taking out your unhappiness on your family members.

It may be hard to get your family to sit down for a meeting. It helps if everyone agrees to the idea of bringing their gripes to a meeting, too. And meetings should be short — nobody wants to sit around for hours trying to solve all the family's problems at once. Talk the idea over with your parents and siblings, and see if they won't agree to try it out. (A "sibling" means a sister or a brother.)

Also, if you like being a "boss," look for other situations where you can be in charge. Start a club with your friends and get yourself elected president. Then you can be the boss of the club. Play school with your younger brother or sister. You be the teacher. Now you're legitimately in charge. See if you can get on the school safety patrol or student council. That will put you in a position of authority too. Help out on the playground, if your school will allow it, or help coach the little kids.

If your new older stepbrother or stepsister is being too bossy with you, tell him or her to lighten up. If your stepsister is boasting because she has a later bedtime or more privileges, tell her to stop it. And if she doesn't, take your complaint to your parent or stepparent — or to the next family meeting.

(But stop and think: Is this the same way *you've* always treated your younger sister or brother? Now that you see what it's like to be bossed around by an older brother, do you think your younger brother or sister liked the way you treated him or her? Maybe now you'll go easier on your younger brother or sister… and that will make the family a nicer place for everyone!)

Sharing Dad

▼ ▼ ▼

Austin and his dad had always been very close. Even after the divorce, Austin saw a lot of his dad. Dad took an apartment very near the house where Austin and his sister and their mom still lived. Not only did Austin, his sister Madison, and their dad see each other at least one day during each weekend, Dad also saw Austin during the week.

Sometimes he took Austin out for a burger. Sometimes he took him to a ball game. Sometimes they went to a movie. Sometimes Austin just brought his homework over to his dad's apartment and did it over there.

Then Austin's dad started dating. After a while, he met a woman named Bonnie. And finally one day, he told Austin he was going to marry Bonnie.

Dad moved into Bonnie's house after the wedding. Bonnie had two kids. "They're your stepsister and stepbrother now," Dad told Austin.

Austin didn't feel related to Tom and Darlene, but he shrugged his shoulders. He didn't suppose it made much difference either way. But soon enough, he saw that it did.

For one thing, Dad had less time to spend with Austin. He still saw a lot of him, but not quite as much as before. Dad was busy with his new family.

Also he didn't live quite so nearby now, so it wasn't as easy for him to get together with Austin.

Austin began to resent his new stepbrother and stepsister. It was their fault that his dad didn't have quite as much time for him. And that's not all! *They* got to be with his dad every day. Austin and Madison weren't with him every day. That didn't seem fair at all!

The way Austin saw it, he and Madison were Dad's *real* children, but they saw Dad only about three times a week. Tom and Darlene were "only" Dad's *step*kids, but *they* got to enjoy being with Dad *every* day. It wasn't fair!

Sometimes when Austin and his sister, or just Austin alone, were going to spend time with his dad, Dad brought Tom and Darlene along. Now Austin was having to share Dad even when it was his turn to be with him. Dad would take the three or four of them out for burgers instead of just taking Austin alone or taking Austin and Madison. Dad would take all of them bowling, instead of just taking Austin or Austin and his sister. "It'll be more fun for you with other kids there," Dad said. "They're closer to your age than Madison is. It'll be better."

But Austin didn't think so. He didn't like sharing his dad. These other two kids had *his* dad to themselves all week, *and* they were cutting in on Austin's little bit of special time with him too.

▲ ▲ ▲

Of course, there's nothing Austin can do about his new stepbrother and stepsister having his dad to themselves most of the week. But if Austin doesn't want to share Dad with the kids on visiting days, he can speak up and say so. Not in front of the kids, of course, but he can say it privately to his father.

Austin probably can't have his father to himself, or to himself and Madison, all day for every single visiting day. Chances are, his dad will still include Tom and Darlene *some* of the times he's with Austin. Maybe Bonnie, Tom and Darlene's mom, will have to go somewhere, and Austin's dad will need to keep an eye on the kids. Then he would have to bring them along when he visits with Austin. Maybe sometimes he just won't want them feeling left out. But probably he could bring them along *less often*.

If he didn't resent Tom and Darlene for taking Dad's time, Austin might eventually find that they're not bad kids. He might find that he enjoys being with them. But first he has to talk to his dad. Without whining or making a fuss, he can say something like this: "Dad, I get to see less of you now than ever. I want to make the time count when we're together. I'd like it if it were just us, one on one, as often as possible, or just you and me and Madison, like the old times."

Chances are, his dad could arrange to include the other two kids less often, even if he can't leave them home every time.

Austin will have to get used to sharing his dad with his new stepsiblings. He feels his stepsiblings are competing with him for his dad's time and attention. And his dad may be going out of his way to make friends with Tom and Darlene, because he's doing his best to make things go well in his new family.

It's true that Tom and Darlene are with Dad when Austin and Madison are not, but that's not their fault. In fact, it's not *anyone's* fault. Austin needs to realize that his stepsiblings aren't deliberately trying to "hog" his dad or horn in on Austin's time with him. The sooner he understands that, the sooner he can get adjusted to the new way things are.

"Us" and "Them"

▼ ▼ ▼

Tyler and Allison's mother just remarried. Mom's new husband, Gordon, is a widower with four kids from his first marriage. Now, since Tyler and Allison's mom got married to Gordon, there are six kids living in the house.

Gordon's kids tend to stick together, unless one of them has a friend visiting. This is true of Tyler and Allison too.

Tyler and Allison feel outnumbered. "There are four of them and only two of us," they complain. They say this new situation makes them feel uncomfortable.

▲ ▲ ▲

Of course they're uncomfortable. Their new jigsaw puzzle family is a big change in their lives. And they're making it worse by thinking of the family as divided into two groups: "us" and "them." It would be so much better if they could think of the six kids as "all of us." It wouldn't be easy, and it will take time, but imagine how much better they would feel if they could start thinking of themselves as one family.

This is nothing they can force on themselves, but there are things they can do to help it along. For instance, they could find something to do that they think their new stepsiblings would enjoy doing, then invite the four of them to join them. Do the kids all like to play sports? They all could shoot hoops, or play soccer, or ride bikes, or even play a simple game like balloon volleyball. How about getting their parents to rent a movie, popping some popcorn, and all enjoying the movie together? What about playing a board game like Parcheesi or Clue or Monopoly or Scrabble together?

If Tyler and Allison and Gordon's four kids start playing games and doing other activities together, they may find that they actually enjoy spending time together. This could be a good beginning. It could start them thinking of "the six of us" instead of "the two of us and the four of them."

There will always be some ways Tyler and Allison will be different from Gordon's kids. When Gordon's kids go to visit their grandma, Tyler and Allison probably won't go with them. When Tyler and Allison spend weekends with their father, Gordon's kids probably won't go with them. (Although, if the family tries to blend all the parts together, it could be even more fun and less confusing!)

But the six of them can stick together most of the time. Or they can do things in smaller groups that are not "us" and "them." Allison and two of Gordon's kids could go bike-riding together, for example, or work on their backyard garden together. Tyler and Gordon's other two kids could play a computer game or skateboard together. Maybe Tyler or Allison will be in the same class at school with one of

Gordon's kids, and they can hang out together at school, or help each other with homework.

Anything else they could do as a jigsaw puzzle family would help bring them closer together. How about planning a Fourth of July party for a few friends, or a backyard carnival? Or they could all work together to cook dinner one night each week. They could even get together and just talk about what their lives used to be like, and how things are changing.

Certainly Gordon's kids miss their mom, just as Tyler and Allison miss having their dad living with them. If the kids all talked about the way things used to be for all of them, sharing their feelings would bring them closer together. It would also make them realize something they have in common: They would realize that they all miss the lives they used to have with their parents. When they realize they all have similar feelings, it will draw them closer together.

It would be good for the kids to sit down together once in a while and talk about their feelings about being part of this new jigsaw puzzle family. The kids could sit down together — just the kids — or they could involve their parents too. It would also be good for them make plans for their future as a family. They'll probably find out that they have some of the same interests. It's likely that one of the things Tyler enjoys doing is an activity one or two of Gordon's kids would enjoy if they tried it.

In fact, if their ages are similar, chances are they like lots of this same things. Talking together about what they like to do will help them find things they might enjoy doing together. Maybe not all six kids together, but at least several of them. They could plan special events, like a party, or game, or a backyard carnival, or a "topsy-turvy" day. (Some families have fun doing a weird Saturday when they eat dinner at breakfast time, breakfast at dinnertime, put their clothes on backward, and try to talk backward too — like, "Fun is this" for "This is fun.")

When you're trying to fit together the pieces of a jigsaw puzzle family, it helps to start thinking of "all of us," instead of "us" and "them." And the first step is to sit down and talk together. The first step to solving *any* problem is often sitting down and talking.

Points to Remember

• *Your place in the family may change when you become part of a jigsaw puzzle (blended) family. You may not be an "only" anymore. You may not be the oldest anymore. There may be more kids on your new stepparent's side of the family than on your birth parent's side.*

• *It feels just as weird and uncomfortable for your new stepsiblings as it does for you.*

• *It isn't "us" and "them." You're all in this together now.*

• *It always helps to talk it out. And you can always bring your concerns to your parents.*

4

Whose House Is This?

▼ ▼ ▼

Recently, Peggy and Aaron's mom got married again. She married a man who has two kids of his own who live with him — Anna and Jonathan. Peggy and Aaron and their mom moved in with Anna and Jonathan and their dad.

The two girls are now sharing a bedroom; the two boys are sharing too.

It hasn't been easy. Though Anna says she's glad to have a sister, she and Jonathan feel like "outsiders" have moved in with them. And Peggy and Aaron feel they don't quite belong there. They don't feel at home. They feel like they've moved into someone else's house, and it doesn't feel like their home — yet.

Jonathan didn't want to give up any of the space in his room, either. His room was quite full and crowded before Aaron moved into it. Making room for Aaron was difficult. It meant he had to put some of his things into storage in the attic and the basement. It meant having to put his desk into the family room. And it was really crowded after they made room for Aaron's bed and dresser.

As for Aaron, he wound up with less than half the room for himself. Some of his stuff had to go into attic storage too, and he doesn't have enough closet space or storage space for his books and games and models and sports gear.

Jonathan feels resentful of Aaron for crowding into his space and bothering him. Aaron feels resentful of Jonathan because Jonathan has much more than half the room for his things and Aaron has much less than half the room for *his* things.

The girls are having a different problem. Even though Anna welcomed Peggy, Peggy doesn't feel completely comfortable. She feels like an intruder. She feels like she's sleeping in someone else's room and living in someone else's house. Anna has circus wallpaper on her walls. Peggy thinks it's babyish. Anna has two whole shelves of Barbie dolls on display. Peggy doesn't like Barbies and doesn't even like having to look at them all the time. Everything in the room seems to say, "This is Anna's room." Nothing there makes Peggy feel at home.

▲ ▲ ▲

The girls in this case have an easier problem than the boys. At least Anna is trying to make Peggy feel welcome. At least Anna says she's glad to have a sister. There are still times when Anna feels a little strange that someone is sharing the room that's always been all hers. But she'll get used to it. She's off to a good start.

If Peggy had a few things she liked on display on the shelves or on the walls, she might feel more comfortable. Peggy's dad gave her a few ceramic horses, which she keeps carefully wrapped in a box. If Anna would give up some shelf space to Peggy, Peggy could display the horses. Then when she looked around the room she wouldn't see just Anna's Barbies. She'd see her own little horses, too — the horses her dad gave her. That would make her feel more at home!

Unfortunately, neither of the adults in the family has realized that Peggy would feel better with her horses on the shelf. But there are two things Peggy could do about it herself. She could ask her mom or her new stepdad to put up a shelf or two just for her horses. Or she could ask Anna to let her put her horses on a shelf that's already there.

It's good that Peggy hasn't whined or complained. It's good that she hasn't yelled, "It's not fair. There's no room for *my* things!" But there *are* nice ways she could speak up for herself. For example, she could say this to Anna: "Do you like horses? I have some ceramic horses my dad gave me. If there were some room on one of these shelves, I could put them up there. I bet they'd make our room look even nicer."

Notice three things: First, Peggy's referred to the room as "our" room. Second, instead of talking about what she wants — equal space for her things — she's talking about what her little horses could do to help the looks of the room. And third, she says "nicer," telling Anna she thinks the room already looks "nice." She's pointing out the benefits to Anna, not just to herself, if the horses go up on a shelf.

It costs money to put up new wallpaper. Maybe Anna's dad and Peggy's mom can't afford to do it right now. But Peggy could ask. If she and Anna could find a wallpaper they both liked, and the parents had it put up, Peggy would feel more at home. Or they could work with their parents to strip off the wallpaper and just paint the walls. Then Anna and Peggy could each choose two posters to hang. That would help too!

The boys have a more difficult situation to resolve. It's only normal for Jonathan to mind having his already-crowded room moved into. It's only normal for him to mind having to put some of his things in storage. And it's only normal for Aaron to mind getting less than half the room for himself.

What can they do about it?

One possibility — which is up to their parents and might cost more than they can afford — is to create a room in the basement for the boys. They could still sleep in their upstairs bedroom but use the basement room for their games and their study desks. If their bedroom had only their beds and their dressers, it would be much less crowded, and they could each have an equal half. Their basement room would be their special den, where they could go to play games, do homework, listen to music, or read. And again, each boy could have half the floor space. Now they'd have one fewer reason to resent each other.

For that matter, if the parents can afford to build a basement room, they might even let one of the boys use it for a bedroom. Then they wouldn't have to share at all.

It's very possible that their parents can't afford to build a basement room. But the boys could ask. It's worth talking about.

But suppose it's not possible to build a basement room. What else could the boys or their parents do to make living together easier?

One help might be if their parents would get bunk beds. This, too, costs money, but not as much as a whole new room in the basement. Bunk beds would save on floor space. Or the parents could get "loft beds" for both boys and put their dressers under their beds. That would save on floor space too. Once they'd saved some floor space, the boys could work on dividing the room more equally.

Another possible help would be to replace some of the furniture in which the boys store their things. Taller, bigger dressers and cabinets would be good. If the boys could store more stuff in their room, Jonathan could get some of his things out of storage in the attic. Aaron might get closer to half of the room for his things, too.

Jonathan and Aaron probably will still have to share a room. Each boy was used to having his own room before; now that's changed. But they'll get used to it in time. (They really will!) Just as Aaron and Peggy will get used to the new house in time. Eventually it *will* feel like home to them.

As they adjust to living together, Jonathan and Aaron and Anna and Peggy will probably also have to deal with sharing each other's things. Jonathan may want to borrow Aaron's soccer ball when his goes flat. Peggy may use Anna's hair dryer without even asking. Such borrowing may lead to arguments and hard feelings. It's a good idea to talk about this possibility and to set limits for each other before problems come up.

No new house feels like home at first. Even if you just move with your mom and dad from one house to another, the new place is going to feel strange. But eventually it begins to feel like home. Jonathan and Anna's house will start to feel like home to Aaron and Peggy with time, too.

And, in the same way, Jonathan and Anna will get used to having Aaron and Peggy living there. It won't feel so strange. It won't feel so crowded. With time, it will be much more familiar. And if the kids take an active part in making the house a little more comfortable for themselves, they can reach that point of feeling familiar and comfortable sooner.

Brothers Apart

▼ ▼ ▼

Michael and Joel are brothers. For three years, they've lived with just their dad, and the two boys shared a room. Recently Michael and Joel's dad got married again. The woman he married has two sons, Noah and Sam.

The whole family moved into a new, larger house. It has four bedrooms — not enough that everyone can have a room of their own. The parents decided that since Michael and Noah are just a few months apart in age, they should share a room. And Joel and Sam, who are a little less than a year apart, are sharing a bedroom also. The parents said the fourth bedroom would be kept as a guest bedroom.

Michael and Joel feel very strange, living in a new house with new people. And being split up from each other hasn't helped. Their dad explained, "It makes sense to put each of you in with a boy who's closer in age to you. You two each go to bed at different times and have different interests. You'll have more in common with your new stepbrothers."

But Michael and Joel have always been close brothers, even though they're more than three years apart in age. Now they're living with new people in a new house, and they're not even sharing a room with each other anymore! They'd rather be together.

▲ ▲ ▲

There are a number of things the boys can do about their rooms.

• They could whine and complain.

• They could pick fights with Noah and Sam.

• They could ask their parents to change their rooms around so they're together.

• They could live with it and try to adjust.

• They could try hard to make friends with Noah and Sam.

What other ideas do you have? What plan do you think might help the most?

First of all, we know that whining and complaining or picking fights with the other boys would not really solve anything. Their parents would probably either ignore them or discipline them if they tried that. And everyone would be unhappy.

They could go to their dad and new stepmom and explain that there have been too many changes at once, and it would be easier for them — and for the other boys — if they could stay together in one room. Maybe in a few months, when the house seems more familiar, they'll think about changing rooms. But right now, sharing a room with each other would be a comfort.

Or they could get together with their new stepbrothers and talk about their "favorite things" — maybe even make lists. They might be surprised at how many interests they have in common. The two older boys might both find that their lists include shooting hoops, playing videogames, watching auto racing on TV, and eating pizza. The two younger boys might both find that their lists include making cookies, watching football games, playing with electric trains, and collecting rocks. And if each boy discovers how much he has in common with his new roommate, he might suddenly feel a lot better about sharing the room with his new stepbrother.

Another thing they might do is sit down somewhere together and compare notes about "What's the weirdest thing about our new living arrangement?" or "What's the hardest thing about our new living arrangement?" When the boys compare their feelings and their difficulties, they might discover that their new stepbrothers — their new roommates — have feelings very much like their own. And discovering that they have something in common is the first step to feeling closer to each other. They can also compare notes on how each of the boys is coping with his problems. The boys might give each other some good ideas for getting used to the new house, the new family, and the new people they're sharing their bedrooms with.

Figuring out how to adjust to a new house, room, or roommate can be one of the hardest parts of becoming part of a jigsaw puzzle family. It takes time — and some real effort — for everyone in the family to begin to feel comfortable living together.

Points to Remember

• *It helps if you can have familiar things around you to make you feel more at home.*

• *Speak up and ask for what you want. But try to word your requests in a way that makes it seem like there are benefits to the other people too.*

• *You might have more in common with your new stepbrother or stepsister than you realize. Try just talking over your interests or your problems, or even making lists to share. Maybe you like a lot of the same things. Maybe you have some of the same problems and feelings. Maybe one of you even has an idea for how to help the other person feel better!*

5

Your Ever-Changing World

Being part of a newly arranged family takes a lot of getting used to. I've said that before in this book, but it's worth repeating. Besides, there are things to get used to that we haven't talked about yet.

Getting used to changes isn't easy. Just the fact that something is different can make it harder to deal with. We're all most comfortable with what's familiar.

In a jigsaw puzzle family, you have to get used to a new stepparent; you often have to get used to new stepsiblings too. And you may be living somewhere new as well. But that's not the end of the changes, either.

"What's for Dinner?"

▼ ▼ ▼

Tammy lives with her mom but sees her dad every Wednesday night and every other weekend. Her dad recently remarried. Now Tammy has a new stepmom and two new stepsisters.

Barbara is stricter than Tammy's dad or mom. Tammy has found this out the hard way. She went to stay at her dad's house after he married Barbara. Barbara had made pork chops for dinner, and Tammy doesn't like pork chops.

Tammy's dad never made pork chops for her because he knows she doesn't like them. And when Tammy's mom makes pork chops for herself, she cooks some chicken or a hamburger for Tammy. But Barbara's two daughters like pork chops, and that's what she'd made for dinner.

"I don't like those," Tammy announced. "May I please have something else?"

"That's what's for dinner," Barbara said. "You don't have to have more than one bite. You only have to taste them. If you still don't like them, just eat your string beans and your mashed potatoes. That will have to hold you."

"But I *know* I don't like them. Why should I have to taste them?! And I'm hungry. I want a hamburger."

"Those are the rules," Barbara said firmly.

"I don't like you!" Tammy said. And she got up from the table and left the room.

Her dad went to get her. "That wasn't very nice," he said. "You may not like some of Barbara's *rules*, but that doesn't mean you don't like *her*. You hurt her feelings."

"I don't care. She's not nice! I don't like pork chops. I shouldn't have to have even a bite. And I want a hamburger. I'm hungry! *You* never made me taste food I don't like! Neither does Mom!"

"Barbara insists that her kids taste everything she cooks. Just one taste — one bite. That's all. She can't insist that her kids taste everything and allow you to do differently."

"It's not fair. Those aren't *your* rules. This is *your* house."

"It's also Barbara's house, now."

"I don't like Barbara!"

"I'm sure you will when you get to know her better. I want my two favorite girls to get along. Now please come into the dining room and apologize to Barbara."

"For what? *She* should apologize to *me!*"

"Tammy, you're acting bratty — and I know you're not a brat. This isn't like you. You're upset. Please calm down."

"I'm not apologizing. I didn't do anything wrong!"

"To begin with, you left the table in the middle of dinner without a good reason and without asking to be excused. Your mom and I taught you better manners than that."

Tammy finally returned to the table, but she wouldn't apologize. She took the tiniest bite of pork chop and called it "Gross!" That got her another talking-to from her father.

The next time Tammy was due to visit her father, she said she wasn't going. She skipped two and a half weeks of visits. Finally she went to see him again. Dinner that night was spaghetti and meatballs with garlic bread. Tammy liked all that, so there was no problem. But two weeks later, Barbara served broccoli.

Tammy scrunched up her face when she saw it.

"Tammy!" her father said sharply.

She relaxed her face, but she looked at him unhappily.

"One bite. You know the rule now," her father said.

She looked at him and didn't touch the broccoli.

"One bite won't kill you," he said.

Tammy took the tiniest speck of a bite possible. It was enough to satisfy her dad, though.

Three weeks later, Barbara served fish. Tammy didn't like fish at all. "Do I have to?" she asked. But her dad could tell from her tone of voice that she already knew she had lost the battle.

"You know the rule," he said, and Tammy tasted the fish.

▲ ▲ ▲

New foods are another thing to get used to when there's a new stepparent in the picture. You may be used to your mom cooking certain things all the time. But suppose your new stepdad likes other foods. Your mom may start cooking them for him. He may do some of the cooking himself, too.

Suddenly you can't count on having your mom's great meatloaf every Thursday night. But maybe Mom will cook a special chicken casserole for your new stepdad. You'll taste it for the first time and like it very much. Maybe your new stepdad prefers Swedish meatballs to Italian meatballs. You're used to eating meatballs and spaghetti, Italian style. Suddenly he's taking over the kitchen and cooking Swedish meatballs. You think, "Yucckk." You miss your meatballs and spaghetti. But maybe you'll learn just how delicious Swedish meatballs are.

Give it a chance. You never know how you're going to like a new food till you try it. There was a time in your life — believe it or not — when you had never had pizza, either. There was a time — a long time ago — when you'd never had a hamburger or a hot dog. Any food is new the first time you eat it.

It can be fun to try lots of different foods — you don't really want just hamburgers or pizza for every meal, do you? And, since our tastes change as we grow, a food you didn't like last year or even last week might taste OK to you now. Talk it over with your folks. Maybe you can have some of the foods you really like if you'll try some of the foods that are really good for you, too.

Rules, Rules, Rules

Different parents have different rules. You know that from visiting your friends. Some parents are more strict, and some are less so. And some parents are more strict about one thing but less strict about others.

When you have a new stepparent, you may have to get used to new rules. This can be true in the home you live in or the home of a divorced parent you visit. Your new stepdad or stepmom may be stricter than you're used to. Or he or she may be less strict. Chances are, your new stepparent will be more strict about some things and less strict about others.

Different rules is another of the changes that you'll need to get used to when one of your parents remarries. You also may be asked to do different chores around the house. It's easy to scream, "Unfair! I never had to do that before!" But the truth is, life is a series of changes.

Changes happen for lots of reasons. Remarriage is only one of them. As you get older, other things change too. You may have more freedom but also more responsibility. You get new and different chores to do. Your parents may also give you new rules to obey.

When you were five years old and didn't have any homework, you had no rules about homework either. When you got a little older, your mom might have told you, "You have to do your homework before you can watch TV." In the same way, other new situations pop up in your life. And some of these situations, too, require new rules.

Don't think that all the new rules in your life now are because you have a new stepparent. Maybe some of them are just new rules because you're getting older. But even if a new rule *is* because of a new stepparent, try to accept it.

Few things in life are all good or all bad, all pleasant or all unpleasant. The same is true of having a new stepparent. You may have new rules to follow. But you may have new privileges too. You may not be aware of the new privileges. Or you may not think about them. Or you may not realize they're because of your new stepparent.

Maybe your new stepdad told your mom, "I think Lee is old enough now to go to the mall with a friend," or "I think Pat is old enough now to go shopping for clothes without you." Maybe it's your new stepdad who persuaded your mom to let you go to the movies with a friend, without a parent going with you.

You might not even know it was your stepdad who suggested these privileges. And this is the same stepdad you think is so strict because he won't let you talk to friends when they call during dinner!

So, if you're feeling resentful of your new stepparent's new rules, try to get over it. There's probably a good side to the new rules too. You just don't realize that the same person who's stricter about some things is less strict about others.

I know it's tough getting used to new rules. But it's something you'll have to deal with as an adult, too. It doesn't stop when you grow up! For instance, laws change. Laws are the rules we all have to live by. The government is always making new laws and changing old ones.

Second, when you go to work, you'll have to get used to new rules on the job. Different companies have different rules from each other. You'll need to adjust to changing rules whenever you change jobs.

You may already be used to this from school, where different teachers may have different rules in their classrooms. For example, maybe your first-grade teacher let you sit wherever you liked, but your second-grade teacher made you sit alphabetically. And maybe your third-grade teacher arranged the class so the shortest kids were in the front and the tallest kids were in the back.

Rules change. It's a fact of life. You may not like it. And you may not like some of your new stepparent's rules. But you'd better get used to rules changing through all your life.

Here's another situation you might find yourself in: Your new stepdad or stepmom has kids. They have to go to bed at 9:00. Your bedtime has been 9:30 for a year now. But since your stepparent and stepsiblings moved in, you now have to go to bed at 9:00 when they do. And maybe they're not a lot younger than you.

Is it fair for you to have to go to bed half an hour earlier? It doesn't feel fair, does it? But now look at it from their point of view. Suppose you could keep your 9:30 bedtime. Would it feel fair to them that you get to stay up later than they're allowed?

No matter what the rules are, *somebody* is going to object. Somebody is going to think the rules aren't fair. And your mom and stepdad (or dad and stepmom) can hardly have two sets of rules. They can't have one set of rules for her kids and a different set of rules for his kids. That would *really* be unfair, wouldn't it?

So, you're just going to have to get used to new rules. Remember that adults have to get used to new rules or laws too. Remember that some of the new rules may actually be easier. And remember that one of the reasons new rules are tough to deal with is that they're a change.

Many people don't deal with change easily. It's not the new rule itself that's so difficult to handle. It's that so many things are *different* now. There's someone new living in your house — maybe even several new people. Or you're living in "someone else's" house. Quite a few things have changed. And now even the rules you're used to have been changed.

Just remember that you *will* get used to it. It takes time, but you will.

Chores!

▼ ▼ ▼

Patti and Kimberly's dad just got married again. When they go to Dad's house on weekends, their new stepmom expects them to help out in the yard. She expects them to pull weeds, pick vegetables, and trim the hedges with the clippers. She works right alongside the girls.

Patti and Kimberly's mom has a gardener who does all that kind of work. The girls don't think it's fair that they should be asked to do it at their dad's house. They're perfectly willing to do indoor chores. They expect to wash the dishes, clear the table, take out the trash, and help prepare dinner. Those are their chores at home. But not the yard jobs!

At their dad's house, their stepmom takes out the trash. There's a dishwasher — the girls' mom doesn't have one. And the girls' stepmom and dad like to do the cooking and all the food preparation themselves, though they do expect the girls to clear the table. "There's nothing wrong with our asking you to help in the garden," they both said. Patti and Kimberly don't agree!

▲ ▲ ▲

Patti and Kimberly have to accept that their chores are different in their dad's house. But if they could figure out what they object to about working in the garden, it would be a first step toward accepting this new chore. Instead of just complaining that they shouldn't have to work in the garden, they need to figure out what they don't like about it.

Is it just because it's a different chore than they're used to? Is it the weather outside? Is it because they don't like to take orders? Do they not like to get dirty? Are they not strong enough to handle the clippers or the shovel?

Maybe it would help if they had a little part of the garden for themselves. They could grow flowers or their favorite vegetables there. If they got used to working on their own gardens, they would grow used to working on the family garden too. Do they mind working in the hot sun? They could try doing their yard work in the early morning, or the very late afternoon, when it isn't as hot and sunny. It also might help if they worked close together and talked or sang or told stories while they worked.

The girls also ought to think about whether the real problem is the kind of chores they're being asked to do. Are the chores the problem? Or are they really upset because their dad remarried? Maybe they haven't learned to like their new stepmom. Sometimes when we aren't happy about something, we don't realize what it is that's really making us unhappy. Maybe the thing that's really bothering Kimberly and Patti isn't the yard work at all. Maybe it's the fact that their dad has married someone who isn't their mom.

It's perfectly normal to feel that way. Now they know there's no chance of their parents getting back together. (There probably never was any chance, but the girls might have still been hoping.) And maybe they feel guilty about being nice to their stepmom. (There's no reason for feeling guilty. It's not disloyal to their mom. But people's feelings often aren't logical.) So maybe the real issue isn't the yard work at all. In that case, the girls should probably talk it over with their dad. Or maybe it would help to talk to their school counselor about their feelings.

If it really is the yard work that they object to, there's something else the girls can do to deal with the situation. Maybe they can *trade* chores. Their stepmom doesn't need them to do the chores they're used to doing, and they don't like the chores they've been assigned. Are there any *other* chores they might be able to trade for? Maybe if they offered to do the family's laundry or make the beds or do the vacuuming or dusting, their stepmom and their dad would accept their doing some of these things instead of the yard work.

Finally, Kimberly and Patti might just decide to do the yard chores and think about having a yard of their own some day. Learning a few things now about caring for their own homes later couldn't hurt!

Are We Having Fun Yet?

Another change when there's a new stepparent is that you may be doing different things for fun. Maybe your new stepdad or stepmom is a bowler. If your mom doesn't bowl, and your dad doesn't either, they might not take you to the bowling alley often. (Maybe you've never gone at all.) If your new stepparent is a bowler, you may suddenly find yourself learning bowling.

Or maybe your new stepparent is into fishing, or likes to play miniature golf, or enjoys photography, or computers, or musical instruments, or.... Here's your chance to learn something new!

Your family might go camping out for the first time. Or, if your new stepparent owns a boat, you might go sailing or water skiing. Perhaps your new stepparent owns an RV. Your family might travel across the country next summer for the first time. These are changes, too, but they're *fun* changes.

Another thing that might be different is your new stepparent's religion. It might be a small difference. You might belong to different denominations of the same faith. Perhaps your mom and you are Lutherans but your new stepdad is a Methodist. That's a difference, but not a huge one.

On the other hand, maybe your family is Jewish and your new stepdad is Catholic. Or maybe your family doesn't belong to any church or temple, but your new stepmom is active in a church. She might ask you to go to services with her one Sunday. Those are big changes.

It's good to learn about different religions. It helps people understand each other better. Too many big wars between countries and small fights between people have been started over religion. By all means, learn something about your new stepparent's religion. You may be asked to join that church or temple, but you don't have to. Just learn a little something about what that religion believes.

You might be surprised at how many things are the same or similar in your religion and your new stepparent's religion.

Your new stepparent may be serious or funny, younger or older than your mom or dad, more strict or less so, interested in different things, or different in other ways. Give him or her a chance. Get used to the differences. I bet he or she is a really nice person — one you could grow to love in time. And I bet there are lots of good things he or she can do for you, show you, teach you. I bet you can have lots of good, new experiences with him or her. Just give it a chance.

Points to Remember

• *There's a lot to get used to when there's someone new in the house. Many people don't find changes easy to deal with.*

• *Your new stepparent's rules may be stricter or more lenient than your parents' rules. Probably some of the rules will be more strict and some more lenient.*

• *You may also need to get used to new foods, new chores, new ways to have fun, and other new things. Try to keep an open mind. You may like many of your new experiences.*

• *If you aren't happy about some of the changes, try to figure out what's bothering you. Is it just because things are different? Or is there something about the new rules or new situations that specifically troubles you?*

• *Sometimes when we think we're upset about one thing, what's really bothering us is something else. You might think you're upset about the changes in your family's rules or bedtimes or dinner menu, but you're really upset because one of your parents married someone else.*

6

Serious Concerns

▼ ▼ ▼

Jonah's parents got divorced when Jonah was seven. A year later, his mom met Jerry. Not long after that, Mom and Jerry got married.

Jerry tried to be a good stepdad to Jonah. "What do you like to do?" Jerry asked.

Jonah answered, "I like baseball. I like to go to the games at the ballpark. And I like to practice pitching and catching my softball."

Jerry offered to take Jonah to the ballpark. But Jonah said, "No, thanks."

Why? Because Jonah's dad used to take him to the ballpark before the divorce. (He still saw Jonah, but he didn't take him to the ballgames anymore.)

It was bad enough that Jerry had moved into the house where Dad used to live, but now he was trying to do "Dad stuff" with Jonah. It felt to Jonah as if Jerry was trying to replace Dad.

No matter which of Jonah's interests Jerry tried to share with him, Jonah said No. Jonah didn't want to practice throwing and catching a softball with Jerry. Jonah didn't want to go to the ballpark with Jerry. When Jerry offered to take him to the carnival, Jonah said "No, thanks," to that too.

His dad had always taken him to the carnival. He didn't want Jerry doing it. Jerry was trying to replace his dad!

Now he began to think this whole mess was Jerry's fault! Maybe if it wasn't for Jerry, Mom and Dad would still be married! And if Jerry weren't married to Mom now, she could marry Dad again!

▲ ▲ ▲

Even though there's a lot that's wrong about Jonah's thinking, it's normal for kids whose parents are divorced and remarried to think the same way Jonah does.

Let's look at where Jonah (and lots of other kids in jigsaw puzzle families) made mistakes:

• First of all, it's not Jerry's fault that Jonah's mom and dad got divorced. Jonah's mom didn't even know Jerry then. And even if she had known him, that still wouldn't make the divorce his fault. Jonah's mom and dad got divorced for reasons that have nothing to do with Jerry — or with Jonah.

• Second, even if Jerry weren't married to Jonah's mom, that doesn't mean that she would want to remarry her ex-husband. It is *very* rare that an ex-husband and ex-wife get married to each other for a second time. And it's even more rare that such marriages work out. Usually whatever was wrong between a man and woman remains a problem. The second try at marriage doesn't work out any better than the first.

Most people try to fix a marriage before they give up on it. People don't just say, "Well, I'm not happy. This isn't working. Let's get divorced." They try to make the marriage work, first. If they have kids, the kids may not know all this. They may not know their parents are unhappy with each other and with the marriage. They may not know that the parents are talking about how to make the marriage better. Kids may not know anything is wrong until their parents say, "We have something to tell you. We're getting a divorce." But it didn't happen that suddenly.

And when a marriage doesn't work between two people, it's not likely to work any better if they try again. Most people know that, though. That's why so few divorced people get married to each other again. (That's also why, when a divorced couple remarries each other, it often ends up in another divorce.)

So, you see, even if Jerry weren't in the picture, Jonah's mom probably wouldn't marry Dad again. (And if she did, and they wound up getting divorced a second time, that would be even harder on Jonah.) Jonah is wrong to feel that Jerry is keeping Mom and Dad from getting back together. Jerry isn't the reason they got divorced in the first place. And Jerry isn't the reason they're not getting back together. So, Jonah shouldn't hold it against Jerry that "Now Mom and Dad will never get back together."

• Last, Jerry isn't trying to replace Jonah's dad. Jerry knows that Dad will always be Dad. But fortunately, Jonah can have both a dad and a stepdad. And if Jonah likes playing ball, or going to ballgames, or going to the carnival, or doing other things, why shouldn't he do them with Jerry? Yes, Dad used to do those things with him. Yes, Jerry is offering to do "Dad things" with him now. But Jerry isn't trying to *replace* Dad. Jerry is just trying to be a good stepdad.

Maybe Jonah feels that he'd be disloyal to Dad if he did those fun things with Jerry. But that's not true! Especially when Dad isn't even taking Jonah to the ballgames anymore. (Anyway, there's no reason Jonah couldn't go to some games with Dad and some games with Jerry.)

Remember, your stepdad or stepmom isn't trying to *replace* your dad or mom. He or she is just trying to be a good stepdad or stepmom. Why not give him or her a chance to do that?

If you have a new stepparent, you are going to be aware of lots of differences between him and your birth dad or her and your birth mom. But the thing that will seem the most different of all about your new stepparent is the fact that he's just not Daddy, or she's just not Mommy.

But he or she isn't trying to be. Your new stepparent wants to love you. He or she wants to be a good parent to you and wants you to love him or her. But your new stepparent isn't trying to replace your birth parent. And when you do learn to love your stepparent, you don't need to feel guilty about it. Love is unlimited. You have enough to go around. You can love your mom and your stepdad and your dad and your stepmom. And your sisters and brothers and stepsisters and stepbrothers too.

So don't resent your stepdad for trying to replace your dad. He isn't trying to do that. He's just trying to find his own spot in your life. The same is true for your stepmom. She wants to be motherly to you. But she's not trying to take anything away from your own mom.

What's In a Name?

▼ ▼ ▼

Alex's mom remarried this year. Now Mom's last name is the same as her new husband, Jason. Jason's kids come and spend every weekend with Alex and Mom and Jason. They have the same last name as Jason, of course. And Alex feels like the odd one out. He's the only one in the family with a different last name. And that makes him feel like he doesn't belong.

▲ ▲ ▲

Alex is thinking about changing his name so he "belongs" to his new jigsaw puzzle family. But does he really want to change his name? Or does he want to keep his dad's name? It's not really an easy decision.

It's possible that Alex's mom can get his last name changed. It's possible that she can't. Let me explain.

When a couple gets divorced, they each get a copy of a legal paper from the court, called a *divorce decree*. It tells some of the things they must do and must not do that have to do with the divorce. Sometimes it's put in the divorce decree that the mother may not change the kids' last names.

If something like that is written in Alex's mom's divorce decree, she can't change his last name. Not unless she gets Alex's dad to agree to it. Then they can get a judge to change what's written in the divorce decree.

If there's not any such thing in the divorce decree, though, then maybe Alex's mom *can* change his last name. Alex needs to ask his mom. He needs to tell her how he feels. Then she can tell him whether it's possible to change his last name. She may not even realize how he feels about having a different last name from everyone else in the family. But if Alex speaks up, she'll know what's bothering him. Then they can discuss whether it's possible to fix the problem.

Even if he can't change his name legally, maybe Alex can still use his stepdad's last name. He would have to use his real last name in school and on any legal paperwork. But he could use his stepdad's last name if he joins the Y or an after-school group, or if he goes to Sunday School with his new stepbrothers, or when he meets new friends around the neighborhood.

Sometimes it's possible to put two last names together. If that's possible for Alex, he might become "Alex Smith-Jones" for example (if his dad's name were Jones and his stepdad's name Smith). Alex will have to give this a lot of thought, and to talk it over with his mom and dad and stepdad. His name will be with him all his life!

"Will You Leave Us, Too?"

▼ ▼ ▼

Lisa's parents got divorced when she was nine. At first, her dad saw Lisa and her brother every Thursday night and every other weekend. She was always happy to see him, but it wasn't enough! She wanted him to move back in with her and Mom.

"I can't, honey," her dad said. "If I could still be living with your mom, I wouldn't have left in the first place. But sometimes things don't work out the way we want them to."

After a year or so, Dad started seeing less of Lisa and her brother, Jim. Some Thursday nights he said he had to work late. Some weekends he said he had to work too. And some weekends he said he was going to be out of town.

Lisa really missed her dad.

Then, when Lisa was eleven, her mom met a man named Barry. Barry was kind and funny and really good with kids. Lisa's younger brother took an immediate liking to Barry. Barry and Jim went jogging together every morning. They rode their bikes together on weekends. They did other fun things together too.

"Why don't you come with us?" Jim asked Lisa. "Barry's really a great guy. I know he's not Dad, but he's all right. You like to bicycle. Even if you don't want to run with us in the mornings, you could bike with us on weekends.

"No, thanks," Lisa said.

Barry tried very hard to be nice to Lisa. He paid a lot of attention to her. He helped her with her homework. (He was much better at History than Lisa's mom was.) He told her funny jokes. He took her to school one morning when she missed the bus, even though her mom said it was her fault. He didn't lecture her about being late, either. But Lisa wouldn't give Barry a chance.

Why not? At first, she didn't think about it. She didn't know why herself.

Then one day, she was talking to her brother. "I miss Dad," Jim said, "but I'm glad we have Barry."

"Don't get too used to him," Lisa snapped at Jim. "He'll just leave like Daddy did." Then she started crying.

Lisa's brother was surprised. Lisa was surprised herself. She hadn't realized she was about to start crying.

Even though it had been a couple of years since the divorce, Lisa still had bad feelings about it. She still felt that her dad had left all of them, and that hurt her. And, although she didn't think about it in so many words, she wasn't going to give Barry a chance to hurt her the same way.

Of course, her dad hadn't really left her and Jim. He had left their mother. Whatever the reason was for Dad's leaving, it had nothing to do with Lisa or her brother. But they were both hurt when he left. And they both missed him.

Jim had been able to accept the divorce more easily. He missed Dad too, but he realized the problem was between Dad and Mom. He missed his dad, but his feelings weren't hurt.

Lisa, on the other hand, was still holding a hurt inside her heart. She still felt deserted. She still felt her dad had left *her*. And she wasn't willing to accept Barry. If she did, and if she grew to love him, then he might hurt her too. One day he, too, might divorce Lisa's mom and move out. But as long as she kept from loving him, he couldn't hurt her. Even if he moved out of the house, it wouldn't matter.

She hadn't thought all this out. She hadn't realized that was why she wouldn't let Barry get close to her. But that was the reason, all the same. She finally realized it the day she broke down crying in front of her brother.

Because Jim really liked Barry, he told Barry what Lisa had said. Barry took Lisa out for lunch that Saturday. He didn't take her out for pizza or fast-food burgers. "I'm taking you to a grownup restaurant because I have some grownup stuff to talk to you about," he told her.

While Lisa ate her special lunch, Barry talked to her. "Your mother was pretty disappointed when her marriage to your dad didn't work out," Barry said. "But it's good to be loved. So when she met me, she took a chance. She knew it was possible that it wouldn't work out between us. She knew it was possible she'd get hurt again. But she took a chance. She gave me a chance.

"I'd like it if you'd give me a chance too. I think you'd like it too. I know you were hurt when your dad moved out. And I'm sure it hurts that he doesn't see you as often as he used to. But just because he and your mom got divorced, that doesn't mean your mom and I are going to get divorced too.

"Are you going to go through life never giving people a chance? Anyone could hurt you. I'm sure you've been hurt by friends. Right?"

Lisa nodded her head.

Barry went on talking. "But you still have friends. Even though a friend or two hurt you, you still gave

your other friends a chance to be your friends...
and one day, when you grow up, you'll meet some
man you'll want to marry, and you'll give him a
chance.

"It might work out. It might not. You might wind
up getting divorced. It happens. There are no
guarantees with love.

"There are no guarantees with any kind of love.
Even with the love of a parent, there are no
guarantees that he'll stay married to your other
parent. Your father will always love you, though. I'm
sure of that.

"And you know what? I love you too. I love you,
and I want to be a good stepdad to you. I just wish
you'd give me a chance.

"There are no guarantees in this world. I can't
promise you that your mom and I won't get
divorced. But I don't think we will. I really think
we're married for keeps. I love her very much... and
I love you very much too.

"You have to take some chances in life. If you
never take a chance, you'll never love anyone. Not a
stepdad, not a friend, not a husband some day. And
that would be a very lonely life.

"Don't even answer me. Just think about it."

▲ ▲ ▲

Barry was right. Life is about taking chances. There are some
chances that it's foolish to take. You don't want to cross in
the middle of the street with heavy traffic coming. You don't
want to experiment with drugs. Those are foolish chances to

take. Loving someone is also taking a chance, but it's a worthwhile chance.

Kids often don't know why their parents got divorced. Or they might know that their parents argued all the time. But just because a mom or a dad gets divorced once doesn't mean it will happen again. Just because your mom argued a lot with your dad, that doesn't mean she's going to argue a lot with your stepdad. Just because Lisa's mom couldn't stay married to Lisa's dad, that doesn't mean she won't be able to stay married to Barry.

Lisa's biggest problem was that she still hadn't gotten over feeling hurt because her dad moved out. She took it personally. She felt he had deserted her. But you know by now that, when a parent moves out of the house, it's not because of the kids. The problem is between the mom and dad. It's not because of anything the kids did.

And the parent isn't really leaving the kids, even though he's not living there anymore. What has ended is his marriage, not his being a dad.

If you're like Lisa, if you keep holding a hurt in your heart, you just make it difficult for yourself. You have to accept that your dad (or mom) *didn't leave you*. And you have to be willing to take a chance on loving a stepparent.

Are There Real "Wicked Stepmothers"?

What about the stepparent who doesn't deserve to be loved? That's a whole different problem. And it's even more serious.

Most of the time, when a mom or dad remarries, they marry someone nice, someone fair, someone worthy of the kids' love. You might think your new stepmom or stepdad is too strict. You might think he or she has some faults. (But don't we all have some faults? You do too. So does your mom, and so does your dad.) You might think he or she is too serious, or teases too much, or has some dumb rules. But really, basically, he or she is an OK person.

But what if that's not the case? What if your new stepparent is really, truly mean to you? I don't mean just strict — I'm talking about *mean*. What if your new stepparent hits you (more than just a quick spank)? What if your new stepparent is cruel to you in some other way? Or what if your new stepparent touches you on a private part of your body?

Tell someone. And if they won't do anything about it, tell someone else. Tell your mom and dad. And if necessary, tell someone else: your grandmother, a teacher you trust, or the school nurse or counselor, or your minister, priest, or rabbi. Or even a police officer.

Just remember there's a difference between being *strict* and being *cruel*. If your new stepparent gives you cruel punishments, for example, that's something to tell about. If she just makes you go to bed earlier than you think you should, that's not being cruel.

Cruel is not just unfair, or disagreeable. Cruel is hitting or hurting you, or forcing you to do things you know are wrong, or repeatedly telling you you're bad or stupid, or making fun of you in public. Look up "cruel" and "strict" in the dictionary for more ideas about the difference.

Now, what about a stepparent you just don't like? Not one who's mean or cruel or does anything terrible to you. But suppose your new stepparent has no sense of humor, really doesn't understand you, doesn't enjoy doing any of the things you like to do, and isn't warm and loving?

It's kind of hard to love someone like that, isn't it?

Well, nobody says you have to love your new stepparent. It would be nice if you did. But love isn't something anyone can *make* you feel. Love isn't anything you can make *yourself* feel, either. Love has to be earned. And that kind of stepparent isn't going to earn your love.

You still have to respect him or her, though. She or he hasn't done anything wrong or mean or cruel to you. He (let's say it's your stepdad) is probably trying to be a good stepfather to you. And apparently your mom loves him.

So be nice to him. Do what he tells you, as best you can. And if you don't love him, don't feel guilty about it. *It isn't your fault.* It isn't anyone's *fault.* He's not being an unpleasant person on purpose.

And you know what else? Maybe he's just nervous. Maybe he just isn't sure how to act around *you.* Maybe he's just as much thrown for a loop by the new situation as you are. And maybe when he relaxes and gets used to you, he'll be easier to be with and you'll like him better.

But if not, all you have to do is be nice to him and be respectful of him. Nobody can tell you you have to love him. And you shouldn't feel guilty if you don't.

Now what about the other extreme? What about the stepparent who tries too hard to get you to like him or her? What about the stepdad who has activities planned for you and him for your every free moment? What about the stepmom who makes all your favorite foods? What about the stepparent who finds excuses for your misbehavior when you know darn well you deserve to be punished?

Grown-ups are human too. This type of stepparent really wants to be liked or loved by you. Give that person an "A" for effort... and an "F" for going about it the wrong way. But try to understand where the person is coming from. At least he or she is trying hard to win you over.

Don't take advantage. Don't be bratty. Don't break all the rules and think you can get away with it forever. Don't ask for your favorite dinners every night of the week. Understand that your new stepparent is trying hard to please you, but he or she won't want to please you if you're obnoxious. So behave yourself and don't take advantage.

"You're Not My Mom!"

Finally on the subject of stepparents, let's talk about four hurtful words: "You're not my mom!" or "You're not my dad!"

When do these words get used?

- When a stepparent is trying to tell a stepchild what to do.

- When a stepparent is disciplining a stepchild.

- When a stepparent is trying to be loving and caring, but the stepchild doesn't want to accept that love.

- Out of the blue, when a stepchild suddenly feels guilty about the good feelings she or he realizes she's developing for the stepparent.

No, she isn't your mom. No, he isn't your dad. But they *are* stepparents. *Your* stepmom or stepdad. And they'd like to be loved, accepted, appreciated, listened to, respected, and made to feel part of the family.

Remember, your stepparent has times when he or she feels like an outsider, too. Just like you! Maybe the house your stepdad now lives in isn't the house he used to live in. Maybe suddenly having two new stepkids and a new wife is more than a little strange for him too. Think about it. You're not the only one who feels out of place! Adults have feelings, too.

No, he isn't your dad. But don't say that to him. He is still your stepdad and you do still have to respect and obey him. And if you learn to love him, that's OK too. It isn't disrespectful to your father. It isn't disloyal. It's nothing to feel guilty over. (Your father will tell you this if you ask him. And if your father's dead, you're not being disloyal to his memory. He would want to know someone else is taking good care of his son or daughter. He would want to know someone is doing for you all the things he can't do now.)

Ugly Stepsiblings

We talked about stepparents you don't like, but what about stepsiblings you don't like? What about the stepbrother who's a mean tease, the stepsister who's stuck up, or the stepsibling you simply have nothing in common with?

The mean tease may be teasing you because he resents your "horning in" on his family. The stepsister who's stuck up may be telling herself she's better than you because she really resents your being there. (You didn't think you were the only one in the family who's uncomfortable, did you? Different people have different ways of showing it.)

Talk to your stepsibling. Tell him or her that you feel bad about the way you're being treated. Say, "We're in this family together. How do we start being friends?"

I'm not saying that will fix everything. It's only a beginning. But you have to start somewhere. Talk to your parent and stepparent, too. Tell them what your problem is. Let them talk to your stepsibling.

Do something nice for your stepsibling even though you don't like him or her. Remember, she may not always be a pain in the butt. She may just be feeling crowded now that she has to share her room or her house, or her dad or mom, or her life.

And if it's just a case of a stepsibling you have nothing in common with? You play video games; she reads. You like sports; she likes cooking. You're very talkative and friendly; she's very quiet. You love weekends; she loves school. You're often into mischief; she's a goody-goody. You love to go places; she loves to stay home. You have *nothing* in common except for being in the same family.

This can happen with a birth sister or brother too. Being born to the same parents is no guarantee of being alike. But if you always were in the same family, if you grew up together from when you were a baby, you don't notice it as much.

Maybe you can learn from your stepsibling. Maybe she can teach you how to bake or play the guitar or build things… whatever her abilities and interests are. I bet if you sat down and talked to her, you'd discover there are some things she does well that you'd like to learn. Or maybe she can help you with the homework for classes in school.

But even if you have nothing at all in common, that doesn't mean you can't like her — or even love her — eventually. What kind of person is she? Liking a person isn't only about the things you enjoy doing together. Liking a person is about appreciating the sort of person that a person is.

Is she kind? Is she understanding? Does she give you hints about how to get along better with your new stepparent? Is she funny? Is she very honest? Is she helpful? Is she patient? Is she forgiving when you're mean to her? Make a list (on paper or just in your head) of all the good things you can say about her. (Think hard.)

You don't have to love her right away (or ever — though you probably will grow to love her in time). You don't have to be best friends with her. Just learn to get along with her. She can do what she likes to do. You can do what you like to do. She can hang out with her friends. You can hang out with your friends. But you're in this family together now. So learning to appreciate her good points is a good place to start.

Jealousy: The Little Green Monster

There's one more thing we need to discuss about stepsiblings: jealousy. When your new stepbrother starts being really loving to your mom, and your mom starts being loving back to him, how do you feel? When your dad includes your new stepsister on the fishing trips that used to be for just you and him, how do you feel? When your brother shoots hoops with your new stepbrother, how do you feel?

Jealous?

It's very normal. But it's not very good.

Remember, love isn't like a pie. If you divide a pie in half, each piece is going to be very big. If you divide it in eighths, though, each piece is going to be much smaller.

But love isn't like a pie. Your mom or dad or brother or sister can love your new stepsiblings and still have plenty of love left to go around. Plenty of love for you. If your mom grows to love your new stepsister a lot, that doesn't mean she loves you any less. It doesn't mean you're any less important to her.

It's harder for "only" children to share their parents with a new stepsibling or two. "Onlies" never had to share their parents before. But even a kid who has three brothers may resent the new "intruders" who are sharing that child's mother's love.

And if your dad says, "I'm proud of you," to your new stepsister, do you feel resentment and jealousy? Do you wish it were *you* he was saying he's proud of?

All these are normal feelings. But they're not healthy. They're not good for you. Accept the fact that you're only being human. But also accept the fact that you need to get past feeling that way.

Your parent doesn't love you any less. You still have all his or her love that you had before. (And now you have your stepparent's love too. And probably your other parent, as well.)

How Are You Feeling?

It's time to make two more lists. On the first list, write down all the things you feel bad about. Whether you think they're good reasons to feel bad, or whether you don't even think they're good reasons, if they make you feel bad, write them down.

Now write a second list: all the things you feel good about. Start with anything that has to do with your family, but include other things too — having a best friend, having a good teacher, having nice clothes and fun games — anything you can think of.

Go back to the first list. *What are all the things you feel bad about?* Having a new stepbrother you don't like? Having to share your mom with your new stepbrother and stepsister? The fact that your stepdad is stricter than your birth dad? The fact that you have to share your room now and you didn't before? (Maybe not all those things are on your list. But I bet some of them are. And I bet there are others, too.)

Now write down *what you can do to make some of these things feel better.* You'll notice I said "*feel* better" not "*be* better." In some cases, you can't change the situation, but you *can* change the way you *feel* about it. Maybe you can do this by getting other privileges that will feel like a trade-off. Maybe you can do this by just talking to the parent you live with about how you feel. Maybe you can do this by visiting your other parent more often. Maybe you can do this by spending some alone time with your birth sibling or your best friend. Maybe you can do this by getting to know your new stepsiblings better. Maybe you can do this by airing your gripes to your new stepsiblings. ("Hey, if I'm not happy, I bet you're not happy either. What can we do to make things better? We're both in the same pickle.")

Now look at your other list. The list of stuff that makes you happy. What can you do to be even happier? Have your best friend over for more sleep-overs? Learn from your new stepdad how he bakes those wonderful cherry pies? Ask your stepmom to take you out on her motorcycle? Spend more time at the library? Spend more time with your birth dad? Get your brother to teach you how to kick a soccer ball better with your left foot? Buy the racing bike your friend Charlie is selling?

Which of the things on this list are easiest to accomplish? Work on getting them done. Work on making them happen. Work on making yourself as happy as you can be.

And work on the other list too. Try to improve the situations that are making you unhappy.

Now, while we're talking about feeling happy and unhappy, let's close out this chapter by talking about *feelings.* When you find yourself a part of a blended family — a jigsaw puzzle family — you may find yourself flooded with a lot of feelings. And some of them aren't good feelings.

The first and most important thing to do is to recognize what they are. The next thing is to accept that, even though they may not be *good* feelings, and even though you need to work your way through them, they're *normal.* They're *usual.* They're *human.* And the last thing? The last thing is to get over the negative feelings. It isn't easy. And it won't be quick. But you can do it.

First let's look at what some of the feelings are:

Guilt. This usually arises if you start to love your new stepparent and begin to feel disloyal to the parent you feel he or she is replacing.

Anger. This may be directed at the parent you're living with, for remarrying, because you feel she (or he) is being disloyal to your other parent, or because you're angry that she (or he) is making you live with these other people. Or it may be directed at the parent you're not living with, because if he (or she) hadn't gotten divorced from the parent you're living with, this whole "mess" wouldn't have happened. Or it may be directed at your new stepsiblings because they're "horning in" on the parent you live with. Or it may be directed at your new stepparent for trying to take the place of your other parent. (And this is true even if your other parent has died.) Or it may be directed at your new stepparent because now your parents are *never* going to get back together.

Sorrow. Now that your mom or dad has married someone else, you know there's no hope of your parents getting back together. (As I said earlier in this book, there probably never was any hope of that. But now it's obvious.) Feeling sad about that is very normal.

Loss. You've lost having your parent all to yourself and your birth sisters or brothers. Now you're sharing her (or him) with a new stepparent and probably stepsiblings too. Your mom (or dad) is no longer just yours, or yours and your siblings.

Confusion. You have mixed emotions. Your new stepdad is really cool... but if it weren't for him you'd have your mom to yourself. Your new stepmom is really warm and loving... but you feel guilty loving her when you still have a perfectly good mom. Your new stepdad is a great guy... but he's the father of that bratty four-year-old who's now taking up so much of your mom's time. And you're confused about how you can feel such conflicting things all at the same time.

It should help you to know that what you're feeling is very human. Very normal. Very common. (Even though you know you really need to get over it. But it isn't as easy as just telling yourself to "Get over it.")

What to do? First, give yourself permission to be human. To feel these things... for a while. Then work on getting over them. It won't happen overnight. It won't happen quickly. But use all the suggestions you've read elsewhere in this book:

• Make lists to help yourself.

• Talk to your mom and/or your dad and/or your stepparent.

• Talk to your sibling. He or she is probably feeling something similar.

• Talk to your new stepsiblings. They probably feel something similar too.

• Talk to a professional — the school counselor, a psychologist, a clergyperson, or some other person trained to give help with feelings.

• Talk to someone you trust like a teacher or coach or youth leader you're close to.

• Remember to look at all the good stuff that's come out of being part of a new jigsaw puzzle family. Maybe you're a girl with a brother, but you never had a sister, and now you have a stepsister. Maybe your new stepmom cooks or bakes some of your favorite foods that your mom almost never made. Maybe you live in a new house that's nearer to your best friend's house or your school or the skating rink or the library. Maybe it's just good to have a dad-type person in the house again. Maybe your new stepbrother has a cool model train set and lets you play with it. Maybe your new house has a swimming pool or a rec room or an extra TV or a pool table. Maybe your new stepdad tells neat stories or is a golfing expert who can teach you to play or is a whiz at math and can help you with your homework, or is just an all-around great guy.

Maybe things are not so bad after all!

Points to Remember

• *Don't be afraid to let go and love. Just because your parents' first marriage, to each other, didn't work out, that doesn't mean their second marriages won't last.*

• *If your stepparent is someone you just can't love, you should still respect him or her. But nobody can make you love anyone, and nobody should demand that you do. Talk to someone if anyone is hurting you, or being cruel or mean to you, or making you do things you know are wrong.*

• *Don't say, "You're not my mom" or "You're not my dad," even though it's true. It's hurtful. And a stepparent knows he or she is a stepparent, not a birth parent.*

• *If you don't love your stepsiblings, you still might be able to get along.*

• *It's normal to have negative feelings, but you need to try to work them out.*

• *Talk to a professional counselor or someone else who can help if you are still having trouble being comfortable in your new stepfamily.*

7

Let's Review Some Facts

What have you learned from this book?

Here are some of the things I hope you learned and understand now:

• You're not alone. Plenty of other kids belong to "jigsaw puzzle families."

• It's normal for you to have some bumps in the road when you're getting used to having a new stepparent and maybe stepbrothers or stepsisters too. This doesn't mean you're a bad stepchild. This doesn't mean your new stepparent is a bad stepmother or stepfather. It doesn't mean your new stepsiblings are mean or are trying to hurt you. It just takes time to get used to each other.

• If you're having problems getting used to the new situation in your family, talk about it. Talk to friends who have been through the same thing. Talk to your mom or dad. Talk to a teacher you like and trust. (Or the school nurse or counselor.) Just talking about what you're feeling can help. Talking about it to someone who's been through the same thing is even better.

• It's not your new stepparent's fault that your parents got divorced. He or she may not even have known your mom or dad then. Even if your stepparent did know your parents then, the divorce is not his or her fault.

• Your stepdad or stepmom is not trying to replace your dad or mom. You can have both a mom and a stepmom or a dad and a stepdad.

• It's not disloyal of you to love your new stepparent. You can love both your mom and your stepmom or your dad and your stepdad.

• Don't resent your new stepparent because "Now Mom and Dad will *never* get back together." It wasn't going to happen anyhow.

• You don't have to call your new stepparent "Mom" or "Dad." If you want to, you can. You can call both your mom and your stepmom "Mom" if you want to. And if your stepparent is "stepping in" for a parent who has died, there's certainly no reason not to. But you can also use a different special name, like "Pop" or "Mama." Or you can call a stepparent by a name, like "Papa Pete" or "Mama Elaine." Or come up with a cute nickname you are comfortable calling your stepparent by, like "MyLiz." Or just use your stepparent's first name, if that's OK with her or him.

• Give your new stepparent a chance.

- When your mom or dad remarries, she or he will be happier. And that's good not only for him or her but for you too.

- Don't be afraid to love your new stepparent because you worry that this marriage might not last either. Love is about taking chances. And anyhow, it's likely that the marriage *will* work.

- It's normal to be jealous of your new stepparent because you're no longer the main person your mom or dad focuses on anymore, but you — and your parents — will be happier when you get over it.

- Having a new stepparent usually means getting used to new rules. This is true whether you live with the stepparent or just visit on weekends or vacations. All through life, even when you grow up, you'll find that the rules you have to live by change. Change is difficult for lots of people. Try to get used to it.

- If your new stepparent is more strict about some things, he or she is probably less strict about others. Try to realize that.

- When your mom remarries, she will most likely take your new stepdad's name. You may not be able to change your last name even if you want to. But if you're sure you do want to, ask your mom if it's possible. However, if it isn't possible, remember that you're still as much a part of the family as anyone. Don't feel like an outsider. It's only a name. And later in life you may be glad you kept your birth name.

- Having a new stepparent may mean having new stepsiblings (stepsisters and/or stepbrothers) as well. They may live in the same house as you or see you only during visits.

• Try not to think of "us" (you and your sisters and/or brothers and your birth parent) and "them" (your stepparent and stepsiblings). You're all one family now.

• Nobody expects you to instantly love your new stepparent or stepsiblings. But do give them a chance.

• Look for the things you have in common with your new stepsiblings instead of concentrating on the differences.

• If you're not happy with a situation, tell your parent. Some things can't be changed, like the marriage itself. Other things might be able to be changed. Or there might be a way around the problem. Try talking it out.

• Make sure you know the difference between a stepparent who's simply strict and one who's really cruel or truly mean.

• If anyone in your jigsaw puzzle family (or anywhere) is truly cruel to you, or does something wrong — like touching you on a private part of your body — you have a real complaint. *Tell someone!* If that doesn't help, tell someone else.

• You may feel like your family is in pieces now. And you may feel the pieces of your jigsaw puzzle family will never fit together. But give it a chance, and you may be surprised at how nicely the pieces fit and what a pretty picture they make when at last they all come together. It will take time. And it will be worth the time — and effort — it takes.

Resources for Jigsaw Puzzle Families

Websites

http://sfhelp.org/11/resources.htm
http://www.thestepfamilylife.com/LinksStepkids.htm
http://www.bellaonline.com/subjects/4584.asp
http://www.stepfam.org
http://www.mywholefamily.com/
http://www.saafamilies.org/
http://www.yourstepfamily.com/
http://www.stepfamilies.co.uk/
http://www.divorcestep.com/resources/books_kids.html

Books

Non-Fiction:

The Boys and Girls Book About Stepfamilies
by Richard Gardner
Creative Therapeutics Inc., 1985

The Divorce Helpbook for Kids
by Cynthia MacGregor
Impact Publishers, 2001

The Divorce Helpbook for Teens
by Cynthia MacGregor
Impact Publishers, 2004

My Other-Mother, My Other-Father
by Harriet Langsam Sobol
Macmillan Publishing Company, Inc., 1979

*Stepmothers & Stepdaughters: Relationships of Chance,
    Friendships for a Lifetime*
by Karen L. Annarino with Jean M. Bloomquist
Wildcat Canyon Press, 2000

When a Parent Marries Again
by Marge Heegaard
Woodland Press, 1993

What Am I Doing in a Step-Family?
by Claire Gallant Berman
Carol Publishing Group, 1990

Help! Girls Guide to Divorce and Stepfamilies
by Nancy Holyoke & Scott Nash
Pleasant Company Publications, 1999

Fiction:
Lord of the Deep
by Graham Salisbury
Random House Children's Books, 2003

Dive
by Adele Griffin
Hyperion, 2001

Where in the World
by Simon French
Peachtree Jr., 2003

Index